YELLOWBIRD

A TRUE TALE OF THE EARLY SETTLEMENT

OF

TOWN SCHLESWIG

MANITOWOC COUNTY, WISCONSIN

BY

HENRY GOERES

TRANSLATED FROM THE GERMAN IN 1900 BY
PAUL DACHSEL.

NORDWESTEN STEAM PRINT,
MANITOWOC, WIS.

Edited by Ed Majkrzak, Sr. and Brad Vogel

Brad Vogel

Yellowbird: A True Tale of the Early Settlement of Town Schleswig Manitowoc County
2016 Edition Copyright © 2016 Editors Edwin Majkrzak, Sr. and Bradley J. Vogel

First Edition, First Printing, 2016

ISBN-10: 0692806733
ISBN-13: 978-0692806739

Euphrosine Publishing
365 Bond Street
Apt. B411
Gowanus
Brooklyn, NY 11231

Cover: Brad Vogel and Suresh Seneviratne
Cover Image: Original painting circa 1904s by Joseph Schema painted for a family member. Photographic image of painting: Kelly Rene Jelinek. Painting and image used with permission of the Rene and Judy Jelinek family.

For the People of Kiel, Wisconsin

With special thanks to:

Rosemary Mohnsam, Research

Sarah Vogel and Max Ames, Typists

CONTENTS

Author Henry Goeres

THE AUTHOR

Henry Goeres, the author of *Yellowbird*, was born in Germany on May 20, 1846, a son of Bernard Goeres. The family came to the United States in 1856 and located in Plymouth, Wisconsin. A year later they moved to Kiel, Wisconsin where Bernard opened the village's first blacksmith shop.[1]

Goeres learned the painter's trade and followed it until he retired. Henry studied law but was never admitted to the bar. For years he was deputy sheriff and constable, and for thirty years was a notary public. He served as an officer of the Kiel Cemetery Association (as of 1915). In addition, he served many years as road commissioner.

A journalist, he contributed articles to newspapers. He enjoyed compiling facts about early history of Manitowoc County for the State Historical Society (he is shown as a member in 1911). A gifted artist, he hand-painted eggs of noted people of the world, also flower designs of every description. His collection of some eight thousand eggs was on exhibit at the Colombian World's Exposition in 1893. The Kiel Historical Society is fortunate to own a small collection of them.

On January 9, 1872, he married Bertha Frese. They had three sons: Henry; Max, who was a dentist in Kiel; and Theodore, a dentist in Lodi, Wisconsin. The house that Henry and his wife lived in was known as the "Castle of Luxembourg". It was located on the very end of South First Street on 20 acres of land[2]. Besides writing and painting, he enjoyed gardening.

He died in Kiel on April 25, 1927.

---

[1] This was located in the building on Fremont Street that now houses the Kiel Lounge, a structure built in 1858.

[2] This house, the "Schloss Luxemburg" is located at 101 River Terrace (where S. First Street climbs the hill from the bridge and turns around the Belitz Cemetery) and belonged to a Mr. Harvey Leonhard for many years in the late twentieth century. Goeres was said to raise potatoes on the small farm. The farmstead included the area that is now filled with residences along Hillcrest Drive and South First Street, stretching off to Mueller Road.

YELLOWBIRD

Yellowbird is a work of fiction, sprinkled with some truth, about the early settlement of the Kiel area. The plot centers on the Sheboygan River, the Kiel dam, and the nearby Indian Village. The characters, in many instances, were actual Kiel residents except that names have been changed for literary purposes: Mr. and Mrs. Henry Belitz are Mr. and Mrs. Behl; the sawmill foreman, Herman Schlichting is Mr. Schlicht; the character Johanna Schlicht is actually Johanna Schlichting, Mrs. Belitz's sister; and Fritz Fichte, Yellowbird's lover, was actually Fritz Fichten, the man in charge of constructing the Kiel dam. Mr. Henry Goeres wrote the novel sometime between 1880 and 1890[3]. It was first written in German then translated to English by Paul Dachsel in 1900.

---

[3] The original printing was in High German by the Demokrat Presse of Chilton, Wisconsin, a press seemingly associated with the Wiskonsin Demokrat, a German-language newspaper published in Chilton, Wisconsin between 1873 and 1895 or possibly the later incarnation, the Wisconsin Demokrat, which was published from 1895-1917. A 1922 booklet entitled A Great Collection of Original Source Material Relating to the Early West and the Far West lists it as: **Yellowbird**. Ein auf Wahrheit aus der zeit der ersten Anfiedlungen des Town Schleswig, Manitowoc Co., Wis. and dates it to "[ca. 1875]". However, the translated version makes references to the 1881 replacement of the dam in Kiel, as well as the construction of the current Kiel mill – which was built in 1883. A thinly-veiled Henry F. Belitz has also been deceased for "a number of years" (he passed away in 1879) when the book is published, per the final chapter. Descriptions of a thinly-veiled Mrs. Belitz's life following Belitz's death also indicate that some time has elapsed, and her children are described as grown and dispersed around the country. Accordingly, it is likely that the original German copy dates from at least the mid 1880s and perhaps more likely the slightly greater remove of the late 1880s or early 1890s. Additionally, the title of the work, which references "Town Schleswig" instead of Kiel, the actual focus of the work, could be taken as a sign that the original German version was published prior to 1892, the year Kiel was officially incorporated as a village, though it may simply refer to what the Kiel area was technically called when the events in the book take place.

FORWARD

Edwin Majkrzak, Sr.

Yellowbird by Henry Goeres is truly a special book. In terms of the history of Kiel, Wisconsin, there is no other source that provides such an interesting window into the early settler days of Kiel in the 1850s before the Civil War. While the book is certainly a blend of fiction and non-fiction, it contains many tidbits that provide us with glimpses of the characters of that time – including Kiel's founder, Colonel Henry F. Belitz, and Old Solomon, one of the last Native American chiefs in the area.

In my decades researching and documenting the history of Kiel, I have spent a good deal of time trying to see which pieces of Yellowbird are historical facts, which are literary fantasies and which are simply the personal thoughts of Henry Goeres, a creative renaissance man who was actually a child when many of the events described in the book were taking place. I don't know that we know for sure in all cases, even at this point. So I hope that Goeres' book's mysteries will keep Kielites intrigued by their own history – and I hope it inspires future research into the history of Kiel that goes well beyond my own.

Ed

INTRODUCTION

Bradley J. Vogel

Yellowbird first appeared on my radar nearly twenty years ago. I found a copy shortly after I met Ed Majkrzak at the Kiel Community Center at Melvin Ruh's 1998 talk about his World War II experiences in Papua New Guinea. I don't recall if it was the one copy of the book at the Kiel Public Library (which Ed had made available with his own funds) or a copy tucked away in a pile of books in the upstairs bathroom of the Kiel Area Historical Society's Heins House. Either way, I was shocked to learn that there was a book about Kiel – an actual literary work that focused on the early days of the town. Needless to say, I read it with deep fascination.

In succeeding years, I realized there were not many copies of the book in existence. A few copies of the German original are known to be in existence in a few libraries and in the hands of several individuals in the Kiel area. And a number of copies of the 1900 English translation can be found in the Kiel area and at various institutions. But all told, I would be surprised if there are more than 50 physical copies of either version at this time. This realization spurred me and Ed to find a way to bring the book back into publication so that it would not be lost to time.

Around the year 2000, I began re-typing the English translation on a computer, but realized the translation, while seemingly accurate in most regards, was sloppy in format – obvious words were mis-spelled, names of characters were inconsistent for no apparent reason. As with so many things in life, the project took a backseat, however. In the meantime, the Wisconsin Historical Society scanned a digital version of the translation and posted it on its website, a significant boost to access to the book. In 2014, I suddenly had a bit more time, and, working with a great team mentioned in the dedication page, we pushed over two years to put this newly-edited version into print.

Importantly, this is merely a clean-up version of the 1900 translation from German into English designed chiefly to circulate the book to a broader audience – first, people need to know the book exists! The task of a further full and painstaking translation out of the original German (to confirm the 1900 translation) lies off in the distance as an undertaking for some future intrepid soul.

About the Book

Yellowbird is intriguing in that it blends fact and fiction. In this edition, we've striven to help make the relevant facts stand out from the fiction with footnotes to help tell the story of the early days of Kiel. While Goeres disguises many of Kiel's early settlers with thinly-veiled alternate names, it's clear that when the character "Mr. Behle" gushes about music or is critiqued as being a hopeless romantic, the author is actually providing a miniature portrait of Colonel Henry F. Belitz, the man who founded Kiel – whether it is biased, meant to be comical or intended as an accurate depiction, the reader is treated to a glimpse of an otherwise unknowable figure who lived and died several generations ago. In providing glimpses like this, the book serves as a sort of time machine that permits us to travel back into our own past.

So many other aspects of early Kiel are revealed: settlement is only just underway in the area, and the virgin forest still reigns supreme; remnant, lingering bands of Native Americans were still very much on hand; and despite being on the frontier of white settlement, Kiel's early days were tied to international events, such as the failed 1848 revolutions in Europe that spurred many, like Belitz, to seek a new life in the United States. Goeres also drops in anecdotes about the surrounding geography, economic realities and the development of the early settlement over time.

The book must also be situated and assessed in the context of its time, the 1880s/1890s. Its romantic plotline is, not surprisingly, quite melodramatic and Victorian. And the book and its original 1900 English translation are, in a number of regards by today's standards, patently insensitive in their portrayal of Native Americans (even as certain practices, qualities and instances of ingenuity of the Native Americans in the story are held up for praise). We in no way endorse the dismissive portrayal of Native Americans or any other races in the book, but we have not sought to alter the substance of the text, as we are trying to present an artifact of a particular time, place and viewpoint to be assessed and critiqued by any discerning reader.

The book and its namesake character did crop up in Kiel history over time well after publication. Yellowbird is mentioned in the 1928 Kiel High School yearbook rather casually. In 1949, the Kiel chapter of the "Degree of Pocahontas", the female auxiliary of the Improved Order of Redmen, a fraternal order, was incorporated as the "Yellowbird Council No. 15". And in 1954 during the city's centennial celebrations, a dramatic play based on the book was performed. To this day, it remains one of the few literary works that can be said to provide some insight into the history of The Little City That Does Big Things.

In the end, Goeres has provided us with a multi-faceted work: a romance, an international thriller (complete with bounty hunters and a shoot-out), a mystery, a case of mistaken identity, a tale of the Civil War (with an apparent sympathy for the South), a drama, a local history, a series of biographical portraits of historical figures, a source of information about Native Americans in the 19th Century, a collection of gossip, an attempt to display a sense of high German culture, a statement of certain political views and possibly a settling of personal scores. It's quite the tale. And it's a unique way to learn more about Kiel, Wisconsin and many other things. So enjoy!

Brad

THE TRANSLATOR

Paul Dachsel, or Charles August Paul Dachsel, translated Yellowbird from German into English in 1900, and the English translation was printed by "Nordwesten Steam Print" of Manitowoc. The press itself was seemingly attached to "Der Nord-Westen", a German-language newspaper published in Manitowoc from 1855-1860 and, after a hiatus during the Civil War, from 1865-1909.

Dachsel, from what we can tell, cut an interesting figure – but one very much in keeping with the milieu of late nineteenth century Germans in America. He appears to have been a clerk, poet, translator, author, and brewer. Born in 1861, he first appears in an 1881issue of The Nation as "C.A.P. Dachsel", a Milwaukee-based co-translator. of Arthur Schopenhauer's Select Essays. Later, he is shown as a clerk in Milwaukee in an 1888 city directory. In one later source, he is "C.A. Paul Dachsel", the author of a chapbook "A Poetical Version of Jean Paul Friedrich Richter's Speech of Christ and Miscellaneous Poems" which was published in 1898 in Sheboygan, Wisconsin. In 1899, he is listed in one source as author of "Eight years among the Malays", a book published in Milwaukee. He is shown in another source listing publishers from 1900 as an author residing in Sheboygan. By 1905, he seems to be an investor in a Cleveland Brewery, per a small note in American Brewer's Review, and in 1916, he published a poem entitled "Oregon or Utopia Up to Date" in the same publication, showing himself as an Oregon resident. A 1909 publication lists Dachsel as a Portland, Oregon resident and assistant treasurer of the Northern Brewing Company, which ran The Star Brewery in Vancouver, Washington. In 1917, he self-published "The world-hoax, and The disillusioned genius, poems by C.A. Paul Dachsel" in Portland Oregon.

YELLOWBIRD

A TRUE TALE OF THE EARLY SETTLEMENT

OF

TOWN SCHLESWIG

MANITOWOC COUNTY, WISCONSIN

BY

HENRY GOERES

TRANSLATED FROM THE GERMAN BY PAUL DACHSEL

1900.
NORDWESTEN STEAM PRINT,
MANITOWOC, WIS.

I. THE GRAVEL PIT

In a gravel pit near the Sheboygan River, whose banks in those days were studded with dense virgin vegetation, some twelve or fourteen laborers were counseling together. Some of the men had their working jackets on and others were in their shirt sleeves, but all of them appeared to be greatly perplexed about something. They were employed in constructing a road from the city of Sheboygan on Lake Michigan through the good timber land lying between it and the eastern shore of Lake Winnebago. A number of smart and influential businessmen had used considerable diligence in securing a franchise for the projected road from the legislature of the State of Wisconsin.[4]

At that time the city of Sheboygan contained about three thousand inhabitants.[5] Between Sheboygan and Lake Winnebago there were but very few white people living. At long intervals a log cabin of the most modest kind appeared to view. Cultivated tracts of land were rarer still.

A boom was expected in this part of the country on account of the increasing current of immigration from all portions of Europe, especially Germany. In order to build a road and at the same time avoid the heavy expenses connected therewith, a cunning idea was realized in the legislature referred to. It consisted in first securing a franchise for a state road and having good surveyors immediately lay it out. As soon as this was accomplished, the same legislature was asked for permission to have the state road changed into a plank or toll road. Incredible as it may appear, such a permit was granted.

The advantages gained by this manoeuver were considerable, for the officials of the state road had the right, by virtue of their charter, to run the road through any lands without paying a cent for the privilege or for the material used. Nobody, indeed, derived any direct gain from this ruse the object of which was twofold, firstly, to furnish the country about the eastern half of the road with a better connection with the Sheboygan market, and, secondly, to secure to that city the market for a longer period of time.

---

[4] Colonel Henry F. Belitz, founder of Kiel, was one of the forces behind this plank road, the Sheboygan and Calumet. He is reported as a commissioner for the road, which was to run from the Town of Herman in Sheboygan County to Menasha, in 1855. After being incorporated in 1854, the road progressed to Howards Grove by 1856 and to Kiel by 1859. In 1861 (the day before Fort Sumter was fired upon), Belitz also received legislative approval for laying out a road from Manitowoc to Taycheedah. He received updated authorization for the same project in spring 1865 as well. While never completed, it would have passed through Kiel.

[5] Sheboygan's population in 1860, approximately one year later, was 4,271.

Land speculators and owners of mills and stores planned the platting of townsites, and they expected that a good highway from Lake Winnebago to Sheboygan, the marketplace, would bring about a more rapid settlement and enable them to sell at a greatly increased price the lands they had purchased very cheaply.

The government of the various states willingly lent their aid to such enterprises and frequently closed an eye in the granting of franchises in view of the fact that the state became more powerful and opulent by such undertakings. Wealth is power, and the possession of power is the aim not only of men, but also of corporations.

It was in the early part of May in the year 1859[6] that the laborers in the gravel pit found themselves seriously perplexed. The pit lay about twenty miles[7] west of Sheboygan.[8] It was there that the locating of a town bearing the proud name of Kiel[9] - although at the time neither a house nor a path was to be seen - was planned.

Some of the laborers were beside themselves with rage, although in reality only mere trifles were at stake. The cause of the commotion was the theft of all their tools while they were eating their noonday lunch — a deed which none were able to understand. The laborers were in the habit of spending the noon hour in a nearby shed. No one ever thought of taking

[6] Kiel, Wisconsin is celebrated as being founded in 1854 upon Belitz's arrival on foot from Sheboygan through the forest at a waterfall on the Sheboygan River, though Ralph G. Plumb's 1904 book on the history of Manitowoc County says Belitz founded Kiel in 1856 with Ferdinand Gutheil. Bernhard Goeres, father of the author, Henry Goeres, built his home and blacksmith shop in 1858/1859 – which remains standing and is currently home to the Kiel Lounge at 212 Fremont Street. The Native American name for what is today known as "Indian Hill" - site of Kiel's Stoelting House, library and community center, was "Boget Squion".

[7] Kiel is approximately 22.6 miles northwest of downtown Sheboygan as the crow flies.

[8] While it could be any one of the many glacial gravel hillsides around Kiel near the Sheboygan River (Kiel sits on the "Kettle Interlobate Moraine" a moraine of debris wedged between the Green Bay Lobe and the Lake Michigan Lobe of the ice sheet during the Wisconsin Glaciation), this is likely a site on the north side of the river not far from the mill site based on other context clues in the story. Many of these gravel hills were leveled in Kiel itself in the early years of settlement (northeast corner of Fremont and First, for example). Early Kiel settlers are recorded walking to Millhome to work in a gravel pit there.

[9] An early settler in the area, Mrs. Charlie Lindemann, named the area for Kiel, Germany according to the 1954 Kiel Centennial "Red Book". According to Majkrzak's History of Kiel, the little settlement of a few cabins that became Kiel was initially called "Hennen".

his tools with him, as thefts among settlers were almost unknown. Most of the laborers were of the opinion that the whole affair was a practical joke and would be explained satisfactorily before one o'clock. Others attempted to cast suspicion on the enemies of the road and set about looking for tracks of the supposed thieves on the nearby riverbanks. They thought that persons inimical to the construction of the highway had undoubtedly cast the shovels, picks and spades etc. into the stream. One of the laborers took the matter very much to heart. His brand new shovel, the acquisition of which in Sheboygan a few days previously had almost completely exhausted his financial resources, was among the missing implements. Although it cost but a dollar, yet how could he, without great loss of time, procure another shovel even if he should succeed in scraping together another dollar? He appeared to be very much affected and swore loudly, although the others, like all settlers at the time, were as poor as himself.

It soon became clear, however, that all the men were mistaken in their suppositions regarding the absence of their tools, for two Indians came upon the scene from the dense thickets and woods to the north. One of the Indians was carrying all the stolen implements that were tied together with wood fibre, while the other followed close upon his heels and belabored his back by means of a long, stout hickory stick. Arrived at the gravel pit, the whipped sinner threw down his heavy burden, whereupon in the presence of the amazed workingmen Solomon, the chief of the Chippewa Indians[10], administered another chastisement to the malefactor of his own tribe. He threshed him as inhumanely as a brutal man would a mischievous dog.

After finishing the cruel flogging, he turned to the toilers and yelled at the top of his voice; "Whisky given! Whisky gibben! Bad white men — Chippewa Indians neber steal!"

The Indians experience difficulty in pronouncing some of the

---

[10] Chief Solomon was an actual Native American character in pioneer-era Kiel; his dugout canoe is on display at the Sheboygan County Historical Museum. The trail that runs between Kiel and New Holstein today is named the Solomon Trail in his honor. While this book denotes the Native Americans involved in the story as the Chippewa, the 1850s was a time of fracturing and blending among the Native American tribes living in Wisconsin as eastern tribes were pushed ever further westward and as settlement from Europe and the East Coast continued. In Ralph G. Plumb's 1904 book "A History of Manitowoc County", it is noted that "In the southwestern part of Manitowoc County also there was a band of Menomonees, under the leadership of a chief named Soloman, which maintained a planting ground in Schleswig as late as 1859." This reference, while rendering the exact tribal affiliation of the Native Americans in the book cloudy, does confirm the fact of Solomon and his tribe's presence in the area. The Pottawottami were also recorded as living in the area at this time. Solomon ultimately passed away at Keshena on the Menominee Reservation.

consonants, especially "B", "F" and "V".

During the transaction Mr. Schlicht[11], the foreman, had joined the men, as the hour for resuming work had arrived, and attempted to secure an explanation from the infuriated Indian chief.

Solomon was very well known and liked by the settlers, since despite his lack of civilization he was a very reasonable man and knew how to control the members of his tribe. The chastised Indian was perspiring profusely and observed with his black, sparkling eyes every motion of his chief. He was by no means craving for a second edition of the punishment he had just undergone, although he had during the procedure neither uttered a sound nor contorted a muscle.

It was ascertained that the Indian had bought a bottle of the poorest quality of whisky for twenty five cents and in payment had given the rumseller a five dollar note. In this transaction the latter cheated the Indian to the extent of two dollars. As most Indians have no idea of numbers, it was no great trick to cheat them with the paper currency that, in those days, was almost the only legal tender circulating, not only in the Northwest[12] but in the whole country.

After the Indian had called at a store, also a miserable hut, to purchase some tobacco, the fraud was discovered. The Indian returned to the rumseller who denied having cheated him. The Indian became enraged

---

[11] While the preamble in the version of this book at the Kiel Public Library in the 1990s indicated that Schlicht is the stand-in for Reinhard Schlichting, brother of Mrs. Belitz, who served with Henry F. Belitz in the Civil War and married Belitz's daughter, there is an instance where Schlict is addressed later as "Herman" by Fritz Fichte. Thus, it seems Schlicht is actually the stand-in for Herman Schlichting. Ed Majkrzak's *History of Kiel* (Revised Edition) records Herman Schlichting, along with Kiel surveyor Christian Tiedeman, collecting $39.00 in November 1856 to construct the first iteration of the bridge across the Sheboygan River in Kiel. The book also lists Herman Schlichting as a millwright who built one of the early homes in Kiel on the southwest corner of Mill Road and Water Street. Reinhard Schlichting is, however, mentioned in the book as an assistant manager of the sawmill, with Fritz Fichten as manager. Zillier's 1912 History of Sheboygan County lists Herman Schlichting as sister of Johanna Schlichting and a founder of the Sheboygan Turnverein (and indicates that he is still alive at the time in Houghton, Michigan). In 1860, Herman Schlichting was appointed road commissioner to establish a road from Kiel toward Lake Winnebago.

[12] In Goeres' lifetime, Wisconsin and the states that make up what we consider the "Upper Midwest" or Great Lakes region were still known as comprising the "Northwest", as they had once comprised the Northwest Territories (addressed in the famous "Northwest Ordinance" passed in the 1780s by the states under the Articles of Confederation), which marked the northwestern corner of the United States at one point prior to the Louisiana Purchase and further American expansions westward.

and drank until he was intoxicated. True to his Indian nature[13], he then took vengeance on the deceitful white men by stealing the implements of the laboring men. In order to fix the fraud beyond any doubt, it was decided to hold court in the tavern that very evening. In order to do justice to the honest chief, the laborers hailed with delight the decision, for they could, without losing time, attend the session which promised to be very interesting. The chief dismissed the sinner who, merry as a king, disappeared in the thicket.

---

[13] Goeres' characterizations of Native Americans - whether resulting from personal experiences with lingering Native Americans in the Kiel area, an attempt to delineate a different, non-European set of values, sheer stereotypes or a desire to throw a sop to readers – are far from politically correct or sensitive to the eyes of a contemporary reader. The words used throughout to describe Native Americans are often unfortunate, although in some instances Goeres does praise certain qualities of indigenous people - and it is often the characters Goeres most desires to ridicule that express the worst stereotypes.

II. YELLOWBIRD

The laborers had lustily resumed their task. The Indian chief was about to take his leave in order to visit a peddler or fur trader, when a pretty Indian girl approached on horseback. She was called Yellowbird, because she was fleet as a bird and her tint was yellow instead of red. Without paying the slightest attention to the laborers or their foreman, she galloped up to them and halted her pony a short distance from them, whither the chief upon her wink had followed her. A moment later they were earnestly conversing together. After a few minutes Yellowbird rode away as hastily as she had come and halted close to the riverbank near a building that was destined to become a sawmill[14].

Solomon returned to the laborers and asked them whether any of them recognized the object that Yellowbird had just brought him. The object in question was a plumb-line, a long cord attached to a leaden ball, a simple contrivance to determine the vertical condition of posts and masonry. None of the laborers claimed to be or to know the owner of the plumb-line.

In the meantime, Yellowbird had ascertained the owner; she had not been mistaken in her first supposition. The plumb-line belonged to Fritz Fichte[15] who was approaching Yellowbird.

Fritz walked leisurely beside the pony carrying Yellowbird who had an air as though she was the ruler of the United States and said to the men in faultless English: "It is not always the Indians' fault when there is trouble between them and the whites. One of our tribe has been punished like a dog for a wrong committed by either a white man or a white woman."

---

[14] The original sawmill built in Kiel in 1859. Belitz had applied for Dam Rights from the state in 1854 before he even owned title to the land. Belitz originally planned to have a gristmill built later across the dam from the sawmill, but it would never come to be (see *History of Kiel* for more). As with many instances in the tale, it's unclear how far the sawmill under construction stands from the gravel pit where the laborers are working.

[15] This is the stand-in for the real life Fritz Fichten, a shipbuilder from Germany hired by Belitz to build the dam and sawmill in Kiel in the 1850s. He was later manager of the sawmill. Not much more is known about him. Interestingly, given Goere's admiration for high German culture, it is possible there is some extra meaning here, as "Fichte" could also be a double reference to Johan Gottlieb Fichte (1762-1814), a major figure in German philosophy and the development of German idealism.

There was a tinge of sarcasm in the accent she placed on the word "woman". Continuing, she said: "The plumb-line which I brought was stolen from the gentleman some time ago. Caqua Mensequaw[16] found it in his hunting pouch without having a suspicion how it got there."

"But Yellowbird!" Schlicht interrupted her; "We are certainly not responsible for that. Do you consider any of us capable of having perpetrated that knavish trick?"

"But if it should be proved that one of your people, a gentleman or a lady, had committed this base act, in order to cast suspicion on we Indians, would he or she have to endure even half the punishment meted out to Mensequa?" Yellowbird asked.

Mr. Schlicht replied: "Caqua suffered the blows not on account of the plumb-line, but for taking away the implements wrongfully and thereby throwing the laborers into great perplexity. Every white man would have been reported and punished, in a humane manner of course, for such an act. For a white man, however, after convicted of a crime, the severest punishment is the disgrace to be suffered, a penalty imposed upon him by his sense of honor; a sensation unknown to the Indian."

"Ha! According to your idea, then, the Indian is sensitive only to kicks and blows. Do you come to this conclusion from the action of the chief toward Caqua but half an hour ago?" Yellowbird asked.

"Your chief," Schlicht replied, "has made many friends by that action. As it is, the old man is respected and honored by all the whites who know him. Even our children like his company. His ideas of right and wrong, however, he has learned from the whites. Caqua, for instance, has but very faint ideas of justice, for otherwise he would not have wreaked his vengeance on innocent laborers for the fraud perpetrated upon him by the seller of fire water."

"The Indians," Yellowbird replied, "are not to be civilized in a day. You, Mr. Schlicht, ought to know that it is one of the Indian's peculiarities to regard the whites as one large family, or as a big, deceitful gang, and what he did, he did in complete intoxication. The mischievous drink, however, which put him into that condition, was given him by a white man for much money – and that man also defrauded him. But this does not by

---

[16] This name and variations of it are littered in Kiel history. An addition to the original plat of Kiel drawn out at some point prior to 1872 is, to this day, known as "Manequa Addition" and consists of the land that is today everything on the south side of Fremont Street from Sixth Street to Third Street, going back to the Sheboygan River. An 1879 bird's eye drawing of Kiel shows Menesqua's "encampment" in this area. A Native American of this name was living in the vicinity of Rockville was also murdered by a young Otto Brachtvogel in the 1870s. The spelling of the name varies through the 1900 translation, e.g., "Mensequaw" and "Mensequa".

any means determine who stole Mr. Fichte's plumb-line. I do wish that you, Mr. Schlicht, would make some efforts to discover the thief."

Schlicht was pleased that Yellowbird brought the matter to a close, as he was well aware of his intellectual inferiority to the girl and did not care to have this revealed in the presence of the men. He therefore turned to Fritz Fichte who, without having taken part in the controversy, had been standing near them, and addressed him thus: "Fritz, have you no clue who may have played a practical joke with that stupid plumb-line?"

"Yes, Herman, I have an idea," Fichte replied; "but I will not utter it until I know more about the matter." He turned and walked away. After a few paces, he turned to the woman on horseback and said: "I would like to speak a few words with you, Yellowbird; if possible, alone. You will find me at the mill."

"I will be there in a few minutes, Mr. Fichte," she answered. When Fichte was gone, she bent down from her horse toward Schlicht and said to him in a whisper: "If you are sincere in the matter, do not forget to think of your sister Johanna[17]. Even though nothing but a miserable plumb-line is at issue, the matter might yet be fraught with grave consequences." Saying this, she turned her horse to the opposite direction and rode to the mill where Fichte was waiting for her.

While these conversations were being carried on, the Indian chief sat on the ground and stared like an idiot at Yellowbird whom the Indians regarded almost as a divinity. When she rode away he burst into a loud laughter, much as a simple-minded father rejoices over a somewhat clever action of his son.

"Yellowbird heap smart, heap smart," he chuckled. Still laughing, he shook Schlicht's hand and repeated that he would be at the saloon in the evening. The Indian then sauntered away.

---

[17] This is Johanna Schlichting, also a sister of Mrs. Belitz, and her formal name appears to have been Antoinette Schlichting. She was the first teacher in Kiel. She was actually seemingly younger than 18 years of age – several sources indicate she was 14 when she started teaching, and a later chapter indicates she is 16 at the time of this story. She was born in the Town of Sheboygan Falls in 1848, however, so she would have been about 11 at the time of this story. We'll chalk it up to artistic license, as this tale is, after all, a blend of fact and fiction.

III.   THE RIVAL.

"Have you given Mr. Schlicht a hint concerning your suspicion, Birdie," Fritz immediately inquired after Yellowbird had joined him.

"Yes," she replied, "don't you know that wherewith the heart is full, the mouth overfloweth?[18] I do not regret having done so, for it was Johanna and nobody else who placed the plumb-line in Caqua's hunting pouch."

Fritz sat on a timber in front of the sawmill while talking to the Indian girl. It seemed as though he was not pleased by the hint Yellowbird had given to Johanna's brother, Mr. Schlicht.

"I know," Yellowbird continued, "that Johanna loves you above all else, and that she has for a long time imagined that I hold you bound in the fetters of love with a mysterious, demonic power, and nobody can rid her of this delusion."

"Birdie," Fichte replied; "you forget that Miss Schlicht is an educated young lady and utterly impervious to such superstition."

"And you forget, Fritz," Yellowbird responded, "that love breaks all dams. Furthermore, Johanna has barely emerged from childhood."

"But smart, very smart," Fichte threw in hastily; "and very modest. Johanna will never display such weakness. Even though love may break dams, with Johanna Schlicht such has not thus far happened - my word of honor upon it. Either Johanna knows how to control herself in a masterly manner or your supposition is wrong. I have not found that she pays a trifle greater attention to me than to the commonest laborer in the house of her brother-in-law, Mr. Behle[19], where I too reside as long as I am working here."

Lightning flashes shot from the fair eyes of the young Indian girl, for she was not at all pleased that Fritz Fichte did not share her views.

"Well then, Fritz," she replied without showing any emotion; "let us drop the whole matter until you either share my conviction or lead Johanna Schlicht to the altar. However, in order to avoid offering an apology, which, strictly considered, I owe Mr. Schlicht, I will leave this

[18] The Bible, Luke 6:45 or Matthew 12:34.

[19] Fichte refers here to the original log cabin of Colonel Henry F. Belitz which stood on the hill just north of the present day Kiel Mill (generally considered the first European settler-built structure in Kiel and the site of the first Township meeting); Belitz's "Fremont House" hotel, which stood generally on the site of Meurmann Engineering and Dairy Queen was not built until later in the 1850s. Various census records, including the census of 1860, show several non-family individuals living in the Belitz household (it appears some were indentured servants).

region tomorrow. We have made the maple sugar for this season, the squaws have tanned the hides, the furs have been prepared for the market, and nothing hinders the good people from beginning their spring journey to the Wisconsin River[20] - never, if my advice is heeded, to return to this region, where they formerly were absolute masters and whence they are now driven away."

With a dexterity that would have done honor to a cavalryman, she jerked her horse around and attempted to disappear in the forest.

Fritz Fichte, however, divined her intention, seized the reins and spoke to her with emotion: "Yellowbird, let us not part thus, at least not forever, as you have indicated. If you cannot endure the truth about a blameless girl and ask of me to speak ill of a young lady for love of you, then, Birdie, depart in peace, never to meet again."

Fichte calmly took his hand from the horse's bridle and extended it to the Indian girl to bid her farewell.

"What you prize so highly in Miss Schlicht, is her modesty, Fritz," Yellowbird answered with great composure; "You cannot, however, call me modest, for I have overwhelmed you with attention, which hitherto always seemed to delight you. But since I must rightfully assume that thus I have become more and more a stranger to your heart, that I appear bold to you and that your joy was only apparent, and that you now seek to wound me by extolling the virtues of Johanna, it is better that we part and, as you have said, do so forever."

"I accepted your attentions with nameless, unsophisticated joy," Fichte interrupted the girl; "not from one obtruding, but as from my beloved one, from my darling. See, Birdie, I tried to be just in this direction as well, especially towards you."

The Indian girl sat wrapped in her blanket as though she had been carved out of stone. It seemed as though for the moment she could not comprehend what Fritz had uttered. A moment later however, she tossed aside her blanket, leaped from her horse and threw herself upon the young man's breast. Raising her beaming face to his and holding his hands in hers, she exclaimed: "Fitz! Repeat again that I am your beloved one; please let me hear once more the sweet word that it may take deep root in my breast and then I am happy and armed to crush my rival."

"Yes, Birdie, I love you, you are my darling, my all," was Fritz's enthusiastic reply; "you have no rival, at least none that could become a menace to you. This ought to satisfy you. You know that I am not a man of many words and much less a phantast."

Fritz enshrined the young girl in his arm and covered her lips with kisses. Yellowbird apparently reveled in the height of bliss.

---

[20] Native Americans in the greater Eastern Wisconsin region would make localized annual migrations based on available food sources and seasonal weather changes.

"I will accompany you to the fountain," Fitz said, "if you will wait until I get a tin pail, as I wish to bring back some fresh water."

While the young man repaired to the upper part of the mill, the young girl stood beside her horse. She had wound her right arm above the neck of the pretty animal and rested with her back against its body. This attitude revealed the girl's entire beauty. She was dressed like an Indian, but very cleanly and tastefully. Her slender body was encased in a tight-fitting cotton jacket which was adorned on the shoulders with some leather cords and pearls. The rest of the garment was tight and short and decked with two rows of white leather fringes. Her dainty feet were encased in moccasins lined with leather fringes that enclosed her feet and calves as tightly as stockings. Her raven-black hair was simply combed back and wound into a queue the end of which was tied with a red ribbon.

In such an attitude, in the midst of the wilderness, Yellowbird might well challenge comparison with the most fashionable lady. It would be difficult to say whether she was conscious of it. It remains a fact, however, that whenever accident or business brought her to a city, to act as interpreter and protectress of her people, she always coldly and energetically declined all invitations to shows, however tempting they might be. She was no friend of flattery. Dudes and gawks found no favor in her eyes.

None knew who and what she was. No one who knew her believed that she was a real Indian. That she was none was betrayed by her excellent education, although she never essayed to shine with knowledge and accomplishments.

Some asserted that she had been with the Chippewas since her childhood and had been engaged, on account of her striking beauty, for four years with a circus. Others claimed to know that she was German and others again that she was an Italian and very proficient on the piano and violin. But all this was mere rumor. Nothing save that she existed was really known of her. She was never seen to beg and tramp, of which the Indians are fond.

As soon as Fichte returned from the interior of the mill, he took the woolen blanket from the horse and asked Yellowbird to use it as a wrap, for the day was dreary and in Wisconsin the beginning of May is not synonymous with summer. He assisted the girl in wrapping the blanket about her slender body, put his right arm around her waist and then both followed the path leading to the fountain.[21] They were soon, however, compelled to abandon this attitude, pretty as it was. The forest became so dense that Fritz seized the girl in his arms as though she was a mere babe and placed her on the back of her pony which had followed its mistress like

[21] It is not clear where this fountain or spring (perhaps an artesian well) was located.

a lap-dog. Yellowbird laughed at Fritz's action and remarked that she really ought to take him with her as hostler, for no one had ever before helped her into the saddle with such gallantry.

Fritz strode ahead of the pony. The path zigzagged past branches and tree trunks which the storms of many centuries had leveled to the ground. At the fountain Fritz once more spread out his arms and laughingly told the girl.

"You won't get away without a farewell kiss - or will you first have a fresh drink?"

"You can safely depend on your farewell kiss, dear Fritz," the girl replied hastily; but since I must return home immediately, I would like to speak with you about the stolen plumb-line. Now, since you have declared me to be your choice, I can speak dispassionately about the affair. I will leave it to your decision whether there is cause for suspicion in what I am going to narrate to you. Caqua Mensequaw is really a very stupid fellow. He does not even possess the instinctive sagacity of his comrades. In the presence of women he grows silly and then he can be put up to anything. He is terribly afraid of getting a whipping. But two weeks ago his hide was thoroughly tanned. The portion allotted to him was almost sufficient to kill a horse. The question was about a trap. When it was ascertained that he had lied, he got whipped. Several days afterward, when he had somewhat recovered, he approached my wigwam, creeping rather than walking, and pitifully begged for admittance. Finally he began to weep and lament bitterly. He promised to do for me whatever I wished if I would but hear him. Without saying a word, I stepped out of my wigwam where I found Caqua cowering like a dog. I did not pamper to his mood, but led him to the point and asked him to speak. Thereupon he drew from his hunting pouch the plumb-line and assured me that it had been put there without his knowledge. He begged me to protect him for once, for he was an ill-omened fellow and did not know what the cord with the leaden ball imported. More blows he said, would kill him. The chief had told him that at a further offense he would be chastised with redoubled severity. He squirmed like a worm at my feet. I told him: 'Caqua, you lie, steal and drink fire-water. Such Indians are terribly bad. I have saved you from many a punishment. I have no desire to protect you further, for no reliance can be placed upon you. But relate your story.' His story was as follows: Mrs. Behl had called him into the shanty and asked him to fetch in some wood and water. By way of recompense the good squaw had given him a large plate of food.

Then she told him that she would purchase of him partridges as soon as he could procure some, after three days, if possible. By her fingers she indicated to him what she meant by three. He had then set about hunting partridges and shot a whole hunting pouch full. This was a day prior to the one on which the whites array themselves in fine clothing and I not work. The handsome girl with the pale face[22] was there too and took the game out of his pouch, while the squaw gave him a shining silver dollar. He did not notice the cord. I promised to investigate the matter, and I assured him that he could rely upon me. His happy features convinced me that he did not dread an investigation. As I understand my comrades like a book, I concluded that he spoke the truth. Now when Caqua again took whiskey, which led up to his foolish revenge, I considered it appropriate to mention the occurrence. You know my explanation of it. The handsome pale girl desires to bring us into evil repute. Perhaps I have made a mistake towards Mr. Schlicht, but probably on account of the smallness of the matter not another word will be said about the cord."

Fritz desired to make a reply, but Yellowbird had already pushed back her blanket, extended her arms and cut off his words, saying: "Say naught, Fritz; I cannot endure it. The whole world may lie at the feet of the handsome girl, but you must not praise her. Neither shall you despise her. I admit that I cannot be just to her, since you dwell under one roof together. Come, Fritz, I will give you the farewell kiss. You have made me your bride and as such I will treat you. Come, Fritz, take the promised kiss from your bride. I am expected at home."

Fritz pressed the beautiful, passionate girl to his side. Never before had he kissed Birdie with such warmth and love.

A moment later she had again wrapped her blanket about her, mounted her pony and embraced its neck with her arms in order to thus protect herself from the low-hanging branches of the trees and thicket. The sagacious beast immediately comprehended the position of its mistress and galloped away into the dark recesses of the forest with as much security as a cavalry horse could exhibit upon a paved highway.

For a few moments Fritz kept standing at the fountain and staring in the direction in which his darling had disappeared.

---

[22] Miss Schlicht

IV.   THE TRIAL.

Towards evening of the same day, heavy rain set in, but rain did not prevent Wisconsin forest settlers from taking a walk. The laborers whom we found in the gravel pit were joined by seven others in vicinity and betook themselves at about eight o'clock in the evening to the saloon to attend the private court session in the whiskey case. The saloon was on the other side of the river on the newly-built plank or toll road[23], about a mile east of the projected city of Kiel, and was intended to catch the trade brought by the new highway.[24] It was even now tolerably well-frequented, for in its immediate vicinity a number of men were employed in a gravel pit.[25]   Those laborers who were not settlers boarded at the saloon. This was an unpretentious log cabin. These cabins were built by laying over one another, in the form of a square, logs of equal dimensions. The open spaces between the logs were filled out with thinner logs or wedges and be-smeared with clay after one or two windows had been inserted. The roof was also constructed of logs. A log of a softer quality of wood was split and hollowed and the two halves shaped like a gutter. Such hollowed logs, placed close together with the hollow side upwards, formed the roof. Over the edges formed by the adjacent ends of the hollow logs, other logs, also hollow, were placed in inverted position. The rain which fell on the trough-like logs thus could run to the ground. The saloon in question included several of such cabins. Whenever the business increased, more cabins were built. In the course of time, the tavern had the appearance of a beaver village.

Those days the tavern keepers in the primeval forests of Wisconsin were mostly lazy fellows or adventurers whose lives had been failures. The proprietor of this tavern was a brutal, coarse fellow. It was rumored that he

---

[23] This is the toll plank road to Sheboygan was incorporated as the Sheboygan & Calumet Plank-Road Company in 1851. The road was built as far as Howards Grove, in 1856, and to Kiel,
in Manitowoc county, in 1859. The road ended its toll in 1902. See *History of Kiel* by Ed Majkrzak for more on this topic. Goeres, as mentioned in the About the Author section, was toll collector/commissioner on this road at one point.

[24] The original frontier tavern mentioned here appears to have been at the site of "Brooklyn Corners" and later Larry's Good Time Inn (today, L.T.'s Good Time Inn).

[25] This is very close to the site of The Gravel Pit Sports Bar and Grill, which sits on the former gravel pit where Ehnert Drive is now located, and which is not far from former gravel pits where Karls Sports Terrace is now located and to the north of the Haunted Barn (near Muhs and Baus residences).

had been a dangerous poacher in Germany, his native land.

In spite of the rain quite a number of persons were gathered at the tavern, for the host had gotten wind of the Indians dissatisfaction and busied himself for the past half hour in explaining in his favor the case to those present. In this tavern were also gathered the components of Kiel, for there were already two parties in the township of which Kiel was to become the principal place. The highway in course of construction ought to, in the opinion of the other party, take a more northerly course in order to reach another waterfall[26], but their efforts proved futile. Mr. Behl proved himself superior to his enemies and remained victor.

The assembly in the tavern included, besides the laborers on the highway, those belonging to the opposition party.[27] These had already liberally partaken of whiskey, when the men from Kiel put in an appearance. Schlicht arrived at the inn at half past eight o'clock with his men, greeted those present and at once asked the host whether he had given whiskey to an Indian known by the name of Caqua Mensequaw and defrauded him of two dollars.

The host, relying on his henchmen, answered as brusquely as a loafer that it was none of Schlicht's business, that his answer would be immaterial, for Schlicht and his horde would still consider him guilty. The saloonkeeper continued that whatever the red dog had told Schlicht was of no consequence to him, as well as what Schlicht or the rest of the gang thought of him.

The Indian chief did not understand a word of the conversation between Schlicht and the tavern keeper. He perceived, however, that the latter claimed the victory. Solomon forced his way as well as he could through the crowd and shouted at the top of his voice: "You no good white man, you cheat Injun and heap whiskey gibben!"

The Indian had barely finished his exclamation when the innkeeper leveled a pistol at him and yelled: "Dog! I have laid low many of your ilk!"

Before he could discharge his weapon, however, Schlicht seized the saloonkeeper by the throat and a scuffle ensued in the densely packed barroom as though an empire was at stake. After a portion of the visitors had left the room and there was more space to move about for the contestants, blows and bricks fell like hail. Above the din was heard the

---

[26] The other waterfall referenced is the waterfall at what is today Rockville. The early Town of Schleswig was indeed divided. Originally named the Town of Abel in 1856 after its first resident D. Able, Belitz and John Barth appeared to have led opposing factions, and Belitz's faction ultimately prevailed, re-naming the township "Schleswig" only a number of months later. Belitz served as first town chairman.

[27] The opposition here seems to be supporters of John Barth.

voice of the host: "An attack, in the middle of the night! Shoot the assassins, I will pay a hundred dollars for every corpse!" He continued to shout in this manner until he was felled by a powerful blow to the jaw.

All of a sudden fire broke out. A candle had been overturned in the vicinity of the whiskey supply and set fire to the spirits. The conflagration spread so rapidly that each one was intent only upon his own safety. While two friends were carrying the battered saloonkeeper out of the tavern, a whiskey barrel exploded. A bluish flame immediately shot out of the low roof and in less than two hours the log cabins that comprised the dangerous tavern were reduced to a heap of ashes. The rain, which was pouring down in torrents, could not check the blaze fed by the alcoholic beverages in stock. The boarders had saved what they could of their traps and blankets and sought for shelter elsewhere. The hose had been conveyed to a nearby shed, where two of his chums took care of him. A week later, after he had recovered, he absconded.

In the days following this occurrence there were many wild rumors about a lawsuit and all who had visited the tavern from Kiel that night already imagined themselves in the devil's kitchen. But nothing of the kind happened. The saloonkeeper was too sharp to take any chances. He knew very well that it could easily be proven that he had sold liquor to the Indian, which was prohibited by law under severe penalty. Arson could not be shown, for the first was either accidental or had been started by the Indian chief. What benefit could be received from a long lawsuit, founded at bottom upon a case of assault and battery. Besides, the host had drawn a weapon before any one had raised a hand against him. Then again the selling of intoxicating liquors had given his log cabin the character of a public house, to which every one had access. After the rascal had weighed all points of the matter, he concluded to keep out of court.[28]

The Kiel people had quietly sought their homes after the fray. The night was dark and wet. They were in poor humor, as none of them had intended to injure the saloonkeeper. The rain continued for two days more and caused the stream to rise to such a height that the dam near the sawmill became endangered.

---

[28] Goeres was a legally-minded individual who served as justice of the peace and occasional legal advisor.

V. THE DAM.

The settlers in the vicinity waited impatiently for the completion of the mill in order to get their large supplies of logs cut up into boards which were badly needed for building purposes.

Fritz Fichte, whose original profession was that of a shipbuilder, had developed into a millwright in this country. He was a very practical young man, a veritable Jack of all trades. Although the transportation of freight to this isolated spot was a difficult matter, yet Fichte possessed the necessary tools to repair almost anything. There was no woodwork which his deft hands were not able to do. In his sawmill he had a forge, anvil, coals which he burned from wood, iron steel and tongs, etc. With the anvil, a report like that of a cannon could be produced. Three shots were fired when the settlers were to be summoned to consider serious questions. In case of danger, more than three shots were fired.

During the third night after the rain had set in, the dam broke on the side opposite the mill. On that side the dam had not been completely finished. Since the spring flood, that is the high water caused by the melting snow, was past no danger to the dam was feared. The long-continued rain, however, caused a considerable rise in the river, which broke the dam on the unfinished portion. Mr. Behl, the proprietor of the dam, had posted reliable men as watchers. Fichte also remained awake, although it could not be demanded of him, but nothing could have persuaded him to retire when danger threatened the possessions of his employer.

As soon as the flood carried away a part of the dam, shots reverberated through the darkness. The shooting was done by filling up the aperture in the anvil with powder and placing another anvil or large stone over it. The heavier the latter is, the louder will be the report.

At the first booming of the improvised thunder machine all the settlers who heard it leaped from their couches, because they knew that at that time of the night it meant danger. Fichte, who had prepared himself for everything during the day, acted as gunner. He lit the powder by means of a red hot iron beam and fired shot after shot into the darkness. He ordered a skiff to be loaded with shavings and kindling and rowed to the other side of the river, where a big bonfire was to be made so that it could be seen when assistance came. The shavings under the roof of the mill had remained dry and after the bonfire was blazing brightly, brushwood and branches were laid on. In a short time the entire hill was illuminated and the environs appeared full of life. Lanterns appeared in the forest from various directions. Cries and calls were heard and the bonfire at the milldam acted as a beacon for all who hurried thither to render assistance

Fichte found very soon that the leak in the dam could not be stopped with earth, for the raging torrent carried it away like chaff. On both sides of the break earth and stones were carried away by the flood as though they had been placed there for the purpose. Fichte had called Behl's attention to the danger and advised him to have huge stones piled up at either end of the dam in case of need. But since it could not be foreseen where the dam would break and boulders are hard to handle in wet weather, the precaution was not taken.

Fichte was about to order the oxen taken out of the stables and hitched up to convey stones to the dam when Yellowbird appeared on the scene. "Poor Fritz," she said with accent of pity; "You are wet with rain and perspiration. I heard the very first alarm and have been here before. When I saw what was the matter I galloped back to our camp to notify our chief. Assistance may come any moment. He told me to see to it that loose soil was on hand wherewith to fill the reed sacks which the water will not wash away. We have about on hundred of those sacks, which we use on our journey."

"God bless you, dear girl," Fritz exclaimed and pressed her stormily to his breast, unmindful of the people about him. In order to instruct his men as to what was to be done, he said in a loud voice "To the hill! Dig up loose earth, for Yellowbird is bringing help." It would have been unpleasant to Fiche to be reproached with having planned love scenes in such moments.

Without suspecting the ultimate purpose the men set about doing what was ordered, especially when Behl, who put in a timely appearance, begged them to do their utmost so save the dam.

"Make your preparation, dear Fritz," Yellowbird said very composedly: "pay no attention to me, I hear the people coming."

Fichte drove a strong post into the edge of the break. By means of an iron hoop he fastened to the post a long and strong trunk of a tree. Through the post and the tree he had bored a hole, through which a piece of iron was driven. Three strong men were placed at the thin end of the tree to turn and raise it upon command. Yellowbird had heard correctly. The Indians arrived, their ponies loaded down with reed sacks, which were filled as rapidly as possible with earth. The open ends of the sacks could be closed like an envelope. After the sacks were closed with a wooden pin and carried on wheelbarrows to Fichte's contrivance, Fichte dexterously wound a chain about the filled sacks, which were attached to the thick end of the tree. The three men at the thin end of the lever then could easily raise, turn and direct the sacks. In order to drop the sacks, the men of course had to approach the post, since they had to raise their end of the lever. With motions of his hand Fichte directed the movements of his men until the sacks were landed where he wished. As soon as this moment arrived, he cast loose the chain by means of a pole and the sack was in the depths of the break to fill out a gap. The men saw what was being aimed at and vied with one another in hurrying up the work. As soon as a sack had been lowered, a fresh sack was on hand.

Yellowbird had remounted her pony and gazed like a statue, her blanket wrapped about her, on the scene. Some of the children and young people had put in an appearance and took great delight in keeping up the bonfire. They gathered brushwood and sticks of wood, dried it at the fire, and then cast it with shouts of glee into the crackling flames. Behl ran about like one in desperate straits and exhorted his men to save his own prosperity and that of the environs. The men did what was in their power. The task of saving the dam went apparently well, but from the opposite side the flood carried off large slices of earth. On account of the distance Fichte was able to pilot reed sacks thither. He was compelled to undertake other measures and therefore asked for someone to assume his post and for two others to wade with him through the water, for on the other side, where the current carried away too much land a barrier had to be erected.

There was a momentary silence, for the work in prospect was very dangerous and might induce sickness and even death, especially as their great exertion caused the men to perspire freely, the season was early and the water icy. No one seemed willing to volunteer. The silence was but momentary, however. Yellowbird shouted to the Indians who had squatted about the bonfire and were smoking their pipes. Her voice electrified them. They leaped up simultaneously and rushed towards Fichte, Caqua in the van.

Fichte was about to give the Indians directions as to what to do, he to accompany them, when Yellowbird was at his side and whispered to him: "Stay at your post, Fritz; our children of nature are as sure-footed in the water as on land. Tell me what they are to do and I will translate it into their language."

The Indians leaped into the water and worked their way to the other side of the stream with the agility of sea otters. Although Indians are in the habit of letting their squaws do all the work and confine their efforts exclusively to the chase, yet in this case they willingly offered their services, for it was their idol, their goddess, who wished it. A plank was pushed out to the dangerous spot. It was long enough to rest with one end on the place where Fichte was standing. Six Indians undertook the job. Four of them had all they could do to prevent the plank from being carried away by the torrent. Even old Solomon wished to enter the water, but Yellowbird protested and he desisted. With renewed efforts fresh reed sacks filled with earth were brought and let down on the plank, as far out as the lever would permit, where two Indians seized them with avidity as though their lives depended on them. Yellowbird interpreted to them

Fichte's orders regarding the place where he wished the sacks to be deposited. Her voice was clear and powerful and rose above the din of the roaring river. After half an hour the reed sacks appeared to rise above the break in the dam. The remaining gaps were quickly filled and when streaks of dawn announced thee new day, the dam was out of danger. A loud hurrah answered Fichte's declaration to that effect.[29]

Mr. Behl stepped up to Fichte, whose hand he warmly pressed, saying with a choking voice: "Thank you, Mr. Fichte." Yellowbird thanked and praised her Indians for their successful labors. The redskins were so delighted with her kind words that they danced about her and shouted with glee, like children to whom their mother is dishing out some dainty morsel, Mrs. Behl with two servant girls and Johanna appeared with lunch and hot grog for the men. Yellowbird was again seated on her pony when Fritz walked up to her, stretched out his arms to her and said rejoicing: "Birdie, let me kiss you. Heaven has sent vou. You are twice my Birdie. I shall marry you twice, for you are too precious to be married but once!"

Yellowbird gave him her hand. "I am glad, Fritz," she said, "I am glad on your account. The people in this neighborhood will speak well of you. Your fame will spread further. But now go home. You need dry clothing, you need rest, for your exertions were superhuman."

"Nonsense! Dry clothing?" Fritz exclaimed; I wish to kiss you, to press you to my heart, you angel!"

"You may kiss me," Yellowbird replied, "but you must renounce pressing me to your heart, for, don't you see? I am soaking wet." She accompanied her word with a hearty laughter, in which Fichte involuntary joined.

"But, girl! Why are you wet?" he asked; "it has not been raining for some time, Don't you see the wind parting the clouds?"

Yellowbird again had to laugh at the stunned expression in the countenance of her lover. "But, Fritz" she said; "don't you remember where you are? How could I come to you on this side of the river without getting soaked. The bridge is not yet completed."

"That is true, darling!" Fritz replied; "you have made the trip through the rapid stream (counting on his fingers) one-two-three-four."

Yellowbird interrupted him with her laughter and said: "Now, Fritz, stop! Otherwise you will spoil your angel. I am about to cross the stream a fifth time with my faithful Robin."

Fichte, who was in a rosy mood on account of the glory achieved by his bride, seized her about the waist, lifted her from her pony and told her: "Wet or not wet, I shall kiss and hug you!" Without resting her on the

---

[29] This episode is seemingly based on true events when a three-day rain elevated water levels above the dam.

ground, he hugged and kissed her and set her again on her pony, saying: "Remember that when I shall call on you tomorrow, which I hope will be in a drier condition, the triumph of today will be duly celebrated. But if one of us needs rest and dry clothing, it is certainly you."

"You are right, Fritz," she said; "one ought never to jeopardize one's health. I will now call our chief's attention to the necessity of keeping our men away from liquor, and then, my dear fellow I will hasten to my wigwam. I have asked one of the squaws to keep it warm until I get back. So, farewell, Fritz."

At this moment Miss Johanna appeared with a basket on her arm, gave Fichte her hand and said: "I could not find you anywhere, I have looked for you to express to you my thanks. If the dam would have been destroyed-her voice quivered at these words—my brother-in-law would have been a ruined man, and my sister and her little children unhappy."

"No thanks are due to me," Fritz replied; "they are (pointing to Yellowbird) due to her."

But Yellowbird was on her way before Fichte could finish his words. After whispering to the Indian chief, she guided her pony to the projected bridge some hundred paces distant, and then rode through the stream. All eyes were fixed upon her. It was broad daylight and Yellowbird sat firmly, as though she had been chiseled out of marble, on the back of her horse which slowly swam to the other side and then climbed like a cat up the steep bank, where it soon vanished with its fair and bold rider. The Indians who had returned to the bonfire were rejoiced and laughed to find their queen of, so much admiration.

VI.   MISS JOHANNA.

Miss. Schlicht seemed petrified. She gazed at Fichte whose eyes were following anxiously his beloved Birdie as she was fording the stream.

"May I offer you some lunch, Mr. Fichte?" she asked him; "You are certainly very much fatigued."

Her offer reminded him of the fact that Miss Schlicht had addressed him once before and that he ought to display more gallantry.

"Thank you, dear miss," he said, "I will wait until breakfast, which I expect will be ready by the time I have changed my clothes. I feel chilly and must talk with your brother-in-law, for the work on the dam must not be suspended until the damages have been completely repaired. Besides, I must go to the mill where arrangements can be made to give a better egress to the flood. I think that before noon the river will have fallen considerably."

"Then at least have a glass of grog," she replied, "My sister, too, has been looking for you. Without waiting for Fichte to answer, she took a glass out of her basket, filled it with grog and handed it to Fichte with the remark that it had probably gotten cold before this time. Fichte took the glass out of Johanna's trembling hand and emptied the beverage, which, indeed, had cooled off considerably, without making any remark. His mind was so preoccupied with his heroine did not even notice that Johanna's eyes were filled with tears. After emptying the glass he said to her: "I see Mr. Behl yonder with your sister; accompany me thither; I know not whether I can meet him more opportunely; what I have to tell him is of importance."

They approached the couple and when Behl saw Fichte coming he turned to his wife saying: "Helen, you can now thank him. Here comes Mr. Fichte, our savior."

Fichte greeted the matron in a very friendly manner but cut short the effusion floating on her tongue by remarking that stones and earth would immediately have to be carted to the dam and the reed sacks ballasted with them, in order to completely repair the damage.

"Thanks will not mend the dam; do not forget this Mr.Behl. I have something to look after in the mill. At home we can talk about the rest later on." With these words he walked towards a skiff which was now almost wholly on dry land, a sign that the water in the river was falling. He pushed the skiff into the water, entered it and rowed towards the mill. Fichte was in the habit of regarding his workshop as a kind of sanctuary.

"Fichte is very chary of his words this morning do you not find him so, Henry?" Mrs. Behl addressed her husband who laughed at the question and excused Fichte, of whom he thought a great deal, as Fichte's extraordinary conscientiousness and heroic exertions had caused him to rise still more in his esteem, by saying: "Fichte possesses not only manly beauty, but also the courage of a hero. Besides, he is the most skillful man I have ever met. If he was a ladies' man in addition, he would make a whole village crazy in six week's time. Extreme tenderness is not his weak side, still his heart is soft as butter."

Johanna replied with some indignation: "But, brother-in-law Henry, if you had seen how a little while ago he hugged and kissed Yellowbird, the Indian, you would obtain a different opinion concerning his weak side."

"And, if you, sister-in-law Johanna, had seen how the Indian, Yellowbird, distinguished herself at Fichte's side today, you would find his hugging and kissing her very natural," Behl replied, adding: "Who knows but that the Indian girl is not the cause that we are not paupers today, for my financial resources are exhausted and I could not have afforded to build another dam. Of that I am certain. Such deeds can carry away natures like Fichte's while an artist on the stage may leave him utterly cold. Fichte judges all accomplishments from the standpoint of utility. He himself is certainly a rare, useful and grand member of human society. What could the Indian girl alone, without the practical guidance of the able and energetic Mr. Fichte, have accomplished with her indolent savages? Without Yellowbird those lazy redmen would not have wetted their toes, my dear Johanna. Our men certainly would not have plunged into the raging current head over ears like water rats, as the lazy Indians did. Fichte would have been the only man who would have dared it, for he knows no fear; but what could he have accomplished alone and unaided? Do you also know, that this despised Indian was the first to put in an appearance when the alarm signals were given? And do you know," he continued, raising his voice, "that it was again the Indian girl who knew that her chief had the means of assistance in his possession and brought his men with them here in time?" In a still higher pitch of voice he perorated: "In order to accomplish all this, the Indian girl had to swim thrice, mind you - thrice; in the pitch dark night with her pony across the swollen stream."

"Then indeed, we are under great obligations to the girl, husband!" Mrs. Behl said.

"She does not care for thanks", Behl answered, "merely pay her the respect due a lady, for she is a lady."

In spite of all the praise showered upon the Indian by Behl, Johanna could not suppress the word that Yellowbird would have done nothing of the kind if she had not been over her ears in love with Fichte.

"Then let us bless this love, Behl said in a tender voice; "for it has saved us from ruin." Tears trickled from the eyes of the ladies as well as of Behl.

The ladies gathered up the dishes and got ready to return to the house. The sun had risen and a beautiful morning promised a delightful day. The men, although tired, were hard at work carting stones to the dam. The Indians had resumed their old seats at the bonfire, relit their pipes and were drying their garments. The red-skinned children of nature are able to endure a little more in the line of hardships than civilized men. Behl finally asked them all into his house, entertained them with lunch, presented each with a silver dollar and a pound of tobacco, and reimbursed the chief to his satisfaction for the reed sacks.

Behl's residence was built exactly like the tavern that we described above, with the exception that it was much larger. The chief finally notified his Indians that it was time to return to their wigwams. Their ponies were grazing on the other side of the river. The Indian does not worry about his horses. The animals, which had not been relieved of their bits and saddles, were foraging for bunches of grass. How much more easily the animals could have grazed, if they had been relieved of their bits. The Indians under-stand the nature of his horses as well as his own.

"See, the Indians are returning," one of the laborers remarked to another.

"The foolish fellows," said a third: "hardly are they dry, when they must wade again up to their necks in water to bring over their horses." But the young man had erred grievously. One of the Indians was standing at the river's edge uttered a call. The animals immediately raised their heads, pricked their ears and gazed at an old black mare. The latter walked towards the Indians and the rest followed her example. Arrived at the other side, the beasts hung their heads and permitted the sun to dry their hides. The Indians paid no further attention to their horses, but basked themselves in the genial sunshine and occasionally fondled their tobacco and their dollars. The tobacco they had received from Behl caused them especial pleasure, as they are very fond of the weed. Even the women indulge in smoking. After lapse of about half an hour, when the sun had sufficiently dried their ponies, they mounted and rode away into the forest.

Fichte had in the meantime changed his clothing and appeared at breakfast. He looked somewhat fatigued. After talking with Behl about the most necessary work to be performed, he retired to enjoy a well-earned rest. The ladies said nothing.

VII. THE INDIAN VILLAGE.

The following day was Sunday. The weather was delightful. There was rejoicing among the settlers and happy faces were the rule. On account of the event of the preceding day, even the women were happy, although their immediate wishes did not transcend the modest hope of securing from the new sawmill a board floor for their humble cabins. Such an acquisition was sufficient to fill the hearts of the poor and unpretentious people with gladness.

Mr. Schlicht, an excellent man of good practical sense and great physical strength, was unable to do his share of the work in repairing the break in the dam, because he was confined to his quarters by an injury he had sustained from a stone falling on his right foot. Fichte did not fail to visit him as often as possible and to keep him posted on the progress of the work, for both were great friends.

The Indian village which lay about two miles northeast of Kiel in a dense tamarack forest consisted of eight wigwams which were the scene of considerable activity.[30] The squaws were busy replacing the large number of reed sacks which had been used in stopping the break in the dam. These sacks are woven out of black ash and leather strips, are very durable and extremely useful to the Indians in their wanderings. Into these sacks the squaws pack all their portable possessions. The sacks are loaded so that when they are fastened to the side of the ponies their weight is equal, although the squaws have no idea of a scale. The wigwams are simple, yet warm. They resemble a straw beehive, but are more round. The roofs resting on poles are made of swampgrass so that they are impervious to rain. All these labors are performed exclusively by the squaws. The Indian does not work. Yellowbird generally assisted in the work, doing the finer tasks. On that day, however, she had prepared herself to receive her lover, knowing that Fichte would keep his word. Although in appearance her wigwam differed in no wise from the other, yet its interior was arrayed in a faultless and inviting manner.

The day being warm and beautiful, Yellowbird wore a light colored calico dress of the pattern described above. Exceptionally, she had put around her neck a row of black pearls. Behind her wigwam was another which appeared uninhabited, for neither a papoose nor any other living being was to be seen about it.

Indians pitch their wigwams in the depths of the forest, in the first

[30] For speculation on the exact location of the village, see footnote 45 for some attempted triangulation based on other references and clues in the text.

place, because it is warmer there, and, secondly, because they are there secure from the fury of storms and not in danger of injury from falling trees, as is the case on the shores of lakes and rivers.

Yellowbird was never molested by the other Indians, even when they were under the influence of liquor for they regarded her as their queen. On the other hand, she never attempted to wound their feelings by a vain display of authority or pride. She tried to lighten the burdens of toil imposed upon the squaws and accomplished much in that direction. These poor creatures, who were almost disfigured by carrying heavy loads and on account of poor treatment, grinned with delight whenever Yellowbird approached.

The deep-rooted habits of the old Indians, of course, were not to be changed. Upon the younger generation, however, Yellowbird kept a sharp lookout and frequently made serious use of the whip when she deemed it necessary. Among the youth she had long since introduced the custom of washing their faces and combing their hair as well as bathing and changing their cloths. At the outset the old Indians could not help laughing when Yellowbird insisted on the new order of things, but now the men and boys were proud of the combs they whittled out of bones or hardwood. The Indians are very skillful in carving and many of their combs were quite artistic. When a child proved obstinate to its mother, the latter had but to say "Yellowbird will get angry" and a new spirit animated the child. They did all so as not offend Yellowbird, who demanded of them no slavish obedience, but only respect and attention, and of lack of these she had no occasion to complain. Even a youth of her own age would not have offered resistance when she administered corporeal punishment to him. This very morning she had severely whipped a young fellow.

The hour of Fichte's visit had come and Yellowbird left her wigwam to meet him. She thereby showed her natural disposition for kindness and also prevented the barking of the dogs when a stranger approached the village. She had followed the path into the forest for some two hundred paces when she espied the handsome form of her bridegroom. Fichte was clean-shaven and wore light pantaloons, a yellow waistcoat and a white linen jacket. A little round straw hat adorned his head. In his hand he carried a light cane.

Yellowbird, who was a stranger to prudery, could not restrain herself from uttering a cry of joy and leaping towards him with outstretched arms with the agility of a roe. Fichte stood still as a grenadier and extended his arm to receive the girl of his heart who flew to him saying: "My dear Fritz! How well you look to-day."

"That you are always," he replied, "I knew that on account of the fine weather you would put on your spring robes today, which I have wished to imitate, I desired to be as much like my Birdie as, possible."

He encircled the girl's slender waist with his arm and like two of the happiest of mortals they sauntered towards Yellowbird's wigwam.

"Tell me, Birdie, what is the matter with the fellow who is resting under a tree in the forest close to the trail? He looks as though he was about to be hanged," Fritz enquired.

Without answering him, Yellowbird wheeled about, turning Fritz, whose hand she held, with her and shouted into the forest: "Pona!"

In a moment the young fellow approached and grinned in the manner of the savages. Yellowbird spoke a few words to him in the Indian tongue, whereupon he brushed the dry grass and leaves from his garment and extended as gracefully as he could his right hand to Fichte who gave it a hearty shake. Yellowbird then renewed her conversation with Fichte and the young Indian took his departure. While sauntering to her wigwam, Yellowbird told Fichte that on this very morning she had given the young fellow a flogging. This news staggered Fichte. He did not know his betrothed in that direction.

"You, Birdie - you have threshed that fellow? Such things also you can do?" he said.

"Whether I can," the young girl replied, "you may ascertain from the young people of the village."

"Are you vying with your chief in the domain of administering corporeal punishment? What crime has this hopeful young redskin perpetrated?" Fritz questioned.

Yellowbird answered: "One of the worst traits of our people is the degradation of the female sex which is subjected to the male. The birth of a girl is frequently cursed and it is by no means a rare occurrence that on such occasions the mother is maltreated by the husband. A newly-born female child is frequently murdered in the most brutal manner by her own father solely because of her sex. If the mother does not care to subject herself to severe abuse, she must remain mute in the face of all such outrages. Although the women are compelled to do all the work, yet the Indians regard the birth of a female child as a misfortune and treat the feminine sex accordingly. I have energetically protested against such brutalities. As a matter of course, the boys imitate the brutal actions of their fathers. Our boys, however, know that I abhor such doings. They have learned that they durst not be rough to the girls. Nevertheless Pona enticed his younger sister into the forest this morning and forced her to hold one of her ears, which are decorated with big brass rings, against the trunk of a tree, so that he would use it as a target for his practice with the bow and arrow.

Pona, who is an expert with the bow, probably for an hour shot his arrows into the brass rings without missing his aim. At last, however, this happened and his sister's ear bled severely. I would never have found out about it, if I had not run across the girl. She had to confess all to me, whereupon I ordered the ruffian home to me, stretched him over this bench and gave him a sound flogging."

The lovers seated themselves on a rough bench in front of Yellowbird's wigwam. Yellowbird continued: "As soon as the girl's ear is healed, she, too, will receive her punishment, she knows that she must not submit to being a target. It is a long time since such cases happened in our village and that is the reason why I punish them severely."

Fichte, who still had his arm about his bride's waist, asked her further, what she subsequently did with the fellow. She replied: "I sent him about to help the women, to split wood for the reed sacks."

Fichte again drew her to his breast and kissed her heartily, saying: "You are a good girl and are doing a good work in ameliorating the condition of the oppressed squaws. Without resorting to corporeal punishment, you will not very likely be able to repress the brutality of youth. You might perhaps remit the punishment to the injured girl. She has suffered enough from the fright endured when her brutal brother aimed his arrows at her."

Yellowbird raised up her splendid eyes to him and said: "That is the very reason why she will be punished, and I have made up my mind to punish her severely. She shall not suffer fright and pain to please a fellow being! She even knows that she ought not."

"But, darling," Fritz interrupted; "what have the parents to say in regard to such matters?"

"The mothers," she replied, "have no voice in family councils and the men punish lack of skill only, not brutality, because they themselves are brutal, of which I have narrated examples to you. I assure you, Fritz, that if such a body aimed at his mother and said that he would shoot out her left eye and then hit her right eye, he could make up his mind that he would be kicked and clubbed like a bucky horse. But if he hit the left eye and it went on record as having made a remarkable hit, the fellow would be the lion of the day."

"Birdie, that is cruel," Fichte remarked.

"Yes, cruel," Yellowbird echoed, "cruel but true. The woman is herself to blame for her degraded condition, because she offers no opposition. The wearied stag will fight at last says Schiller[31]."

Yellowbird had committed a lapse of the tongue. She noticed it, but too late. Fichte had leaped to his feet.

"Says Schiller!" he exclaimed; "Birdie, who are you?"

Yellowbird had recovered from her fear and smilingly gazed into his countenance.

"Who and what I am, Fritz?" she echoed modestly; "I am Birdie, you bride."

[31] Joseph Christoph Friedrich von Schiller, German poet, philosopher, playwright and historian (1759-1805).

She tenderly rested her handsome head upon his breast. Fichte placed his hand on the girl's cheek, pushed back her head a little and stared into the depths of her black eyes as though he sought to read in them what she did not wish to confess voluntarily. Yellowbird's smile gradually increased until at length she burst into a loud laughter. Fritz first rapidly snatched a kiss from the lips of the heavenly creature and then laughed with her as loudly as he could.

"Well Fritz! Have you found the rascal?" Yellowbird, still laughing, asked him.

"What rascal, girl?"

"The Schiller," she replied, slapping Fritz with both hands on his yellow waistcoat so that he almost bounded back. He encircled with his hands her round arm near the shoulder and while shaking he in a roguish manner, said "Just wait! You will have to confess, else I will employ your own method. A bench and a whip are quickly to be had."

Fichte at this moment beheld Yellowbird's fine pearl necklace. "Today I am overwhelmed with surprises. I have never before seen you wear these beautiful pearls. I now see that they match you admirably and I must restrain myself that I do not devour you for sheer love."

"None else has ever seen these pearls on me, dear Fritz," she answered; "you are the first to behold them. I had determined not to wear them until I became a bride. It pleases me, Fritz, that you like them. You are interested in them, for without you I would not be a bride."

Fichte inspected the pearls more critically and found that they were of a very rare quality.

"Many questions are vibrating on my tongue," he said, "but I do not wish to torment you. There is no Indian girl on the face of the globe that can display such pearls."

"I will not contest that," Yellowbird replied; "but, there is no Indian girl on the face of the earth with whom you could have fallen in love - it must need be that I am something extraordinary; why should not my jewelry be of the same character? But now come into my castle. We will still have plenty of time to enjoy the fine day out of doors."

Yellowbird pushed back a finely decorated bearskin which hung across the entrance to her wigwam, struck a military attitude at one side of the entrance, bowed low and said laughingly: "Will your highness be pleased to enter?" They entered the wigwam.

"The exterior of your castle does not promise such a splendid interior," Fichte remarked after his eye had roamed about.

"With the splendid interior you must, certainly mean me," she replied laughingly; and me alone, for otherwise I do not see where the splendor could come in, unless you would regard that stuffed raccoon in the corner as an object of beauty."

"All persons who possess the necessary cash can have parlors with modern improvements, carpets and paintings," he said; "but to make a hut like yours so tasty and tidy, that my Birdie alone can accomplish. To prove to you that I intend no flattery, I will seal my just verdict," and, saying this, he drew her towards him and pressed a kiss on her lips.

"Since you have assumed the role of a judge," she replied; "I will at once make you a cup of coffee. You may then criticize my culinary art. If you were to postpone this until after our marriage, it would not be well for you if your critique was adverse."

She wound herself out of his arms to execute her design.

"I protest, Birdie," Fichte exclaimed; "for in the first place I am not accustomed to drinking coffee between meals, secondly, you ought not to trouble yourself doing something I do not care for."

"You will have to accustom yourself to many things before you have piloted me, your wife, to the brink of the grave," she answered, "trouble is out of the question; today you are my guest and I insist on your trying my coffee."

With her small delicate hands she started a fire in the stove. Fichte, not wishing to wound the feelings of his bride ceased his opposition to her wishes. "I would like to ask you Birdie why you alone use a stove, since the Indians are in the habit of maintaining an open fire in their wigwams and roasting their meat on spits?" Fichte asked.

"Have I not alone a pearl necklace?" Yellowbird replied with a smile. She was evidently in very good humor today.

"But how do you transport the stove on your long and wearisome journey?" Fichte continued to query.

She answered: "I do not take the stove and the dishes with me, they stay here."

"But when you stay at your summer resort on the Wisconsin River, what do you do then?" he asked.

"There also I have a stove and dishes," she said.

And how did you manage to get the stove into these forest recesses?" he enquired.

"You are such a good mechanic and cannot explain that?" she said. "Just look a little more closely at the stove."

"I see," said Fritz: "the stove can be separated into at least fifteen pieces."

"And the separate parts," Yellowbird interrupted, "are packed into reed sacks, hung over the backs of the ponies and transported over stumps, stones and streams."

During the conversation Yellowbird had started the fire and put a kettle of water on the stove. The stove-pipes led straight up through the opening at the top of the wigwam. She then began to spread the table. This consisted of a saw-buck, whose parts were held together with buckskin straps. When the legs of the quaint table were spread out, the buckskin serving as the top of the table was tight as a drum. Her chairs were built on the same principle. Fichte was highly pleased with the dexterity and rapidity with which she performed her domestic functions and was fascinated by her chattering.

After Yellowbird had taken a coffeemill from a closet that was shielded from gaze by an antelope skin, she reached into it again to take out a supply of coffee beans. How carefully and skillfully she performed this maneuver, however, she could not prevent Fichte from casting a glance at its interior and surveying its contents.

VIII. SAVAGE OR TEUTON?

A hasty scrutiny of the interior of the closet caused Fichte to exclaim involuntarily: "Child! What books are arrayed upon your shelves!"

Yellowbird blushed as though she had been entrapped into doing something mischievous. But determined as she was in all things, she brushed aside the curtain and said: "Behold! A fine collection for the daughter of a savage, isn't it, Fritz? Here you will find the Schiller, for whom you were a little while ago searching in my eyes, as well as Lessing, Goethe, Shakespeare. They are all here, even Fritz Reuter."[32]

In this region, Yellowbird had never been known to speak any other tongue than English or Indian. All at once she asked Fritz in the most perfect Low German[33] idiom: "Shall I read you something from Reuter, about "Uncle Braesig[34]" (or 'Who Shall Carry over the Pan')?" She accompanied her words with a hearty laugh. Fichte was beside himself for commotion. He stood before the mysterious, fascinating maiden, his breast heaving like that of one delirious with fever.

"Birdie," he exclaimed, "you, a Low German! From the lips of my wild Indian bride I hear in the midst of an American wilderness the dear, bewitching idiom of my home, the language of my parents, and in the wigwam of this Indian girl I find the English and German classics? Birdie, if you have come to us from the realm of the fairies, then be my good angel, for you hold me a prisoner with your celestial charms. But if you are a terrestrial being, then, 0, adored angel! Tell me who and what you are!"

"Yes, my boy you shall know it! I am a Low German girl!" she said in glee, again rushing into his arms.

[32] Gotthold Ephraim Lessing, German writer, philosopher, dramaturg, publicist and critic (1729-1781); Fritz Reuter, northern German poet and novelist (1810-1874).

[33] "Low German" is, depending on whom one asks, either a dialect or a separate language that originated and was once spoken in what is today northern Germany, southern Denmark and parts of the Netherlands. While it remains in use in some Mennonite communities in the United States, it is largely a dead language at this date.

[34] Uncle Braesig comes from Ut mine Stromtid, Reuter's 1864 work loosely translated as "From My Farming Days". The work presents some of the northern German aspects of the revolutionary movement of 1848 in German, a key factor that led many Germans to emigrate and ultimately settle in the Kiel, Wisconsin area.

Fichte slowly sank upon a chair and drew Yellowbird upon his knees, placed his left arm about her shoulder and told her with a tender voice, for he was so moved and fascinated that tears trickled down the cheeks of the handsome, courageous young man: "Birdie, the few sweet homelike words from your beloved lips have taken a boulder, a mountain from my heart. I have been yours a long time past. However, the puzzle of who and what you were, has been torturing every fiber of my existence, though in this land, where all nationalities are shuffled together promiscuously, all puny, philistine national pride is soon lost. But, Birdie," he continued, drawing her more closely to his breast, "you were a savage, even though accident gave you a good education - how and by what means no one could tell - and however beautiful you might be, you were and remained a savage. To be happy with you, child, was out of the question. I did not worry about that, my nameless love gave me sufficient assurance on that score, but if - pardon me, Birdie, if I speak freely, as you yourself have said, 'the mouth overfloweth wherewith the heart is full' - heaven should bless our marriage with children, whom would they have resembled? Instead of inheriting the tender, courageous character of the mother or the traits of Germanic blood, they might have taken after the barbarous monstress of your pedigree, who are capable of aiming their arrows at the eyes of their own mothers! But, child! We are in no such danger!"

Heaving a deep sigh, he placed also his right arm about his jewel and dressed her fervidly to his breast. Her face was almost covered by Fichte's powerful arms. The embrace of his stormy love caused her to exclaim with exuberant delight: "0! 0! Boy, look! Don't you see that I have coffee beans in my right hand?"

Fichte dropped his arms and her sweet, charming features again appeared in full view. That seductive light that glistened in her eyes and defied heavenly glories again united its power with that of her captivating smile. Without changing her position, she raised her left hand and brushed back her blonde locks from her fevered brow. After a while she said: "Fritz, a breach has been shot into the fortress of mystery shielding me. Yet I must continue to defend it valiantly and therefore I pray you, from the bottom of my heart, to be content with what you have learned today. Ask me no further, irrespective of what pictures you may form in your imagination, for you would injure my feelings. Let me tell you that my father was an honest, good, brave Low German sea captain and my mother a foreigner, every inch as good as my father, but no savage. From her I inherited my black hair and black eyes. My complexion is as white as your own. It does not appear so, because I always paint. To do so without damaging my teint, I learned from an American equestrienne, a friend of mine. As it is hard to do business without humbug in this country, she gave herself out as a Creole and carried out the deception successfully by her skill in the use of toilet powder. I received a good education. I speak German, English and French with equal fluency. I have studied music and can play on the piano and violin as well as sing. You will be proud of your wife, whom you can without compunction introduce into the cream of society."

Winding herself out of Fichte's embrace, she arose and said with great emotion: "And the hand which I extended to you as a bride is pure and unsullied." She burst into tears. Fichte's eyes clung to her. He devoured eagerly every word she uttered. She continued: "Fate forced me out of my natural career to a place among the savages in the primeval forests of this strange country. This peculiar fate has compelled me to throw the veil of mystery about me. It is no fault of mine. In due time I will give you a true and faithful account of all."

Drying her tears, she seized the coffeemill and said in a different tone of voice: "Well now let us see whether we are going to have coffee or not," and again she burst into a bell-like laugh.

Fichte remained seated, wiped the perspiration from his brow and the tears from his eyes and remarked: "'I thank you very much for your revelation. I will not ask you to say anything more unless it meets with the approval of your best judgment. My confidence in you is as firm as a rock. I am proud of you and will never knowingly endeavor to wound your sentiments by curiosity or mistrust."

Fichte raised himself to his full height. Joy and bliss beamed and suffused her pantry. She chose it for that purpose, because it was a cooler place for the storing of supplies. After folding together the table and putting the remnants of the feast into a large basket she managed to place unobserved a clean cup from the closet into the basket. Taking the coffee can from the stove, she took it and the basket with her into the adjacent wigwam.

During her absence, Fritz had ample opportunity to observe how wonderfully clean and tidy Yellowbird kept her habitation. Her bed was stowed away in a hammock; her wardrobe was screened by a cotton curtain; the floor of the wigwam consisted of mats of similar make as the reed sacks of the Indians. Fichte had a great desire to inspect several objects more closely, especially the closet containing the library, but he was too noble-minded to do such a thing unbidden. Besides, Yellowbird returned immediately and asked him to determine how the afternoon should be spent and whether he would be pleased to take a walk through the village. Fichte consented to sauntering about with her through the village, especially as he desired to give thanks to the good Indians who had rendered him such valuable assistance. Accordingly, they went into the open and approached the nearest wigwams. Yellowbird was leaning on Fichte's arm. He was impressed by the appearance of the surroundings of the wigwams, for all rubbish, brush-wood and the like had been removed and burned. He knew that an Indian might stumble, a score of times over an obstacle without thinking of removing it. Yellowbird explained to him that she had the boys under her supervision to do the cleaning up. When it was done, the whole village was glad of it, although none of their own accord would ever think of doing so.

"By taking you as my wife I rob the poor Chippewas of their educator and their patron spirit," remarked Fichte.

IX. AMONG THE WIGWAMS.

From the left side of the tamarack forest Pona appeared on the scene with a stick of cordwood on his shoulder. The wood was to be cut into strips of which the squaws wove reed sacks. When he beheld his queen and her companion, he dropped the wood, brushed his garment and leaped up to Fichte with a friendly grin to shake his hand--a somewhat comical affair, over which the couple laughed very heartily. With her left hand Yellowbird drew the boy to her side. He was extremely happy on that account, as was evident from the bright expression in his black eyes, which looked up with devotion to Yellowbird. After explaining to the youth the cause of their hilarity and the significance of a handshake, she dismissed him. Gay as a lark he put the wood back on his shoulder to bring it to the squaws.

The lovers reached the Indian women who had crowded together and were busy weaving sacks. The Indians regarded Yellowbird as a supernatural being whom the Great Spirit had sent them for their weal and salvation. The justifiable mistrust of the redskins towards the whites was never displayed towards Yellowbird, for whom they would have gone through fire.

The squaws were squatted on the ground. They are very fond of shining frippery and baubles, for which they have frequently bargained away much more valuable objects. Their appearance gave evidence of that trait. Rings of pewter wire hung in their ears and every other available spot. Yellowbird had never reasoned against that barbaric and puerile display of worthless tinsel, because she was unwilling to rob the poor creatures of one of their greatest pleasures. Fichte could not help making comparisons between Yellowbird and the ugly creatures. She spoke to the squaws who occasionally as a mark of respect raised their heads and grinned at Fichte. When one of them laughed, they all did the same. Yellowbird knew that Fichte was conversant with Indian traits and therefore paid no heed to the antics of the squaws.

Yellowbird, it appeared, was telling the squaws about the break in the dam and about Fichte, at whom they gradually stared more often. She called to herself the children, among whom were some really pretty faces.

"Don't you think," she asked him, "that if some of these little girls had received my education, they could endure comparison with me?" She had observed what was transpiring in Fichte's mind, hence her question.

"As soon as the poor young creatures are about to enter womanhood, they are smitten with the curse of the red men's brutality."

The girl whose ear had been pierced by Pona's arrow, and an older one appeared before Yellowbird who dismissed the former with a few words which drove the purple blood into her copper-lined face and made her walk away shamefaced. In the meantime Pona reappeared with another stick of cordwood. Yellowbird spoke to him, because she sought to reward diligence and obedience with love. She ascertained from him that Kaan, a bigger boy than Pona, had not obeyed Yellowbird's order to split wood. Pona was immediately dispatched to bring Kaan before her. In a few minutes he stood before her, hanging his head and overcome with shame. She informed him that he could thank the stranger for not getting flogged, and at once Kaan begged for mercy and promised to perform right then not only the neglected work, but much more in addition.

"You will perform the work allotted to you at all events," his stern judge replied; "and when the sun is behind the forest, you will appear at my wigwam and receive the punishment which your disobedience and your indolence deserve. Now go about your work, but first greet our visitor."

Kaan greeted Fichte in the same manner as Pona had done a short time previously and then disappeared in the depths of the forest, where he went to work.

While walking with locked arms towards the other wigwams, Fritz asked her: "Wasn't that sinner No. 2?"

"He begged for mercy," Yellowbird replied.

"Which the stern judge did not grant, for he made that impression on one, when he walked away," Fichte said.

"You have observed correctly, Fritz", she answered; "for if I had remitted the punishment, he would boast of it towards others and my justice would become threadbare and produce an evil impression on the rest of the children. Kaan himself would be spoiled most thereby. I spoke in the Indian tongue to him, as I always do in such cases that the parents may profit by the examples."

"I am astonished at your authority in this village, Birdie," Fichte said; "the fellow whom you have just now sentenced is taller than you. Suppose he would offer resistance to you?"

"If he but raised a hand against me," she answered, "he would not be able to remain with the tribe. Thus highly am I prized."

The dogs came and sniffed, but refrained from barking. The Indians, whose acquaintance we made at the dam, appeared also. The dogs of the Indians do not bark at the approach of strangers when in the company of one of their masters. The Indians shook Fichte's hand, saying: "How do, how do, good white man." Every white man who has done them no injury is a good white man to them.

The Indians squatted at the foot of a tree and gave themselves up to smoking. Some of them polished their rifles, which are furnished them by the government.

Their squaws are never allowed to even touch the guns. Such an act they would consider a desecration of the weapon which is as dear to them as a part of themselves. In furtherance of a treaty, the government furnishes the Indians semi-annually with ammunition, woolen blankets and some currency. The most shameful frauds that, especially in the West, have frequently incited the Indians to bloody uprisings, are often coupled with such transactions. However, the federal officers found it impossible to perpetrate any fraud upon Yellowbird.

The Indians also did considerable whittling and carving. They made very artistic and practical saddles for their ponies, as well as ax handles which are a model for those made in this country to the present day. Their canoes are as well-adapted to their purpose and as finely proportioned as a skilled craftsman could possible make them. The canoes are made of barks or hewn out of the trunks of trees. The latter are selected by the men and felled by the squaws. The assertion has often been made that the squaws build the entire canoe, but that is an error. The canoes are distinguished by their light construction and, like all implements of the Indian as well as American, are exceedingly practical.

When the Indian meets any obstacles in his journeys on rivers and creeks, he puts the craft on his shoulders and carries it across the portage - for miles sometimes.

Chief Solomon distinguished himself by his courteous demeanor towards Fichte. Only one, Caqua, remained at his task, that of whittling a handle for the tomahawk which lay before him.

"Caqua, are you not anxious to see our white friend?" When Yellowbird had uttered Caqua's name, an ugly grin spread over his features and he drew near with canine submission and greeted as his comrades had done before: "How do, how do, good white man?"

What a creature this Caqua was! His fellows were tall and slim, but he was a giant endowed with great physical strength. His face was simply a fright. In battle he had lost a portion of his nose and his whole face was covered with cuts, scars and bruises. His entire body is said to have born similar marks.

Yellowbird conducted Fichte into a number of wigwams to show him their supplies of smoked meat and furs. The latter included the skins of muskrats, beavers, raccoons, foxes, lynxes, otters and skunks. All these animals were caught in traps. The skins of bears, stags and wolves were tanned and, when a surplus stock was on hand, sold. Otherwise, they were used as quilts and blankets. The garments of the Indians were made of buckskin. The Indians were acquainted with the art of tanning from time immemorial. All these labors are performed by the squaws. After the Indian has brought home the results of the chase, he reposes on his couch. The trapping season was over and the Indians were enjoying a good time. In the morning and evening they went hunting for ducks and partridges, of which they brought home a good lot. For wild pigeons[35], with which the forest abounded, and rabbits and squirrels they cared very little. The young people hunted this kind of game with the bow and arrow.

Whenever a young Indian was considered by the federal officers to have arrived at a sufficiently mature age, he received a rifle. Such an occasion was always accompanied by a feast.

Ever since Yellowbird became the queen of the Chippewas, furs were no longer bartered away for useless baubles, since she was well posted on their market value. If the Indians had possessed any ideas of economy they might, as many white hunters and trappers have done, have acquired wealth.

In the meantime Fichte and Yellowbird returned to the squaws. A little girl there came tripping up to Yellowbird who took her by the hand and led her to her wigwam, at which the girl seemed highly pleased. Yellowbird ordered her to fetch some water in a tin vessel from a nearby spring and prepared some raspberry lemonade, of which they all partook.

Fichte was making mental comparisons between the manner in which he and the majority of laborers had spent the Sunday afternoon. His pure and natural pastimes contrasted very favorably with the drinking and cardplaying of his fellows. He handed his glass to the little Indian girl to put away and then asked Yellowbird who had absented herself a moment with the flask and the fresh water and had apparently returned from the mysterious wigwam: "Birdie, if you do not consider it an impudence, I would request you to tell me something about that Indian, Caqua I think you call him. The fellow made a poor impression on me."

Yellowbird burst into a loud laughter upon hearing Fichte's view and said: "I think he makes that impression on everybody. It is, indeed, not to be wondered at. Meeme, fill up again Mr. Fichte's glass. Let us all have some more lemonade."

After they had all drank their fill, she ordered Meeme, the little girl attending her, to return the glasses to the wigwam and then go to assist the other children in taking the shavings their mothers had made while at work into their parental wigwams. The shavings were to serve as kindling. The young girl trotted away in a merry mood, delighted with the attention Yellowbird had bestowed upon her.

"A lovely creature, this little Meeme, but what a peculiar name," Fichte observed.

Yellowbird laughed and said: "Meeme means dove. In our village we have quails, swallows, starlings, finches, even bears, stags, alligators, serpents, wolves, buffalos etc.; Maqua, for instance, means bear. Caqua, of whom I am going to tell you, means monster."

[35] This is very likely a reference to the extinct passenger pigeon, see later footnote for more.

Fichte laughingly said that he found those names very appropriate. Yellowbird began: "Caqua is an outlaw among the savages and is not a member of our tribe, but of the Menominee who have almost exterminated our tribe in endless boundary war. Some three years ago he sent word to our chief, asking whether he could be received into our tribe on condition that he be fettered until the truth of his story be verified. It is an ancient rule of war among the Indians to bind deserters hand and feet and let them hunger and suffer for days until their story can be verified. This procedure is resorted to in order to prevent treachery. Our people accepted the condition and the fellow endured that torture for eight days. After our spies had verified his story, he was free, furnished with food and drink, and has been with us ever since. Caqua is a courageous warrior. He knows no fear. But his boldness is equaled by his cruelty and love of plundering. He received the wounds defacing his body in robbing expeditions. It is said that while beastly intoxicated he stabbed to death his squaw, wherefore he was presented by his tribe. We have also heard that he killed some of the members of his own tribe. When this report reached us, he was sentenced to death, for the Indians do not tolerate a fratricide in their midst. However, I vetoed the death sentence."

Fichte was stunned at her veto power and gazed at Yellowbird with a questioning air.

"Yes, yes, Fritz," she said, "I have the power of life and death in the tribe of the Chippewas. Are you not proud of me?" He said: "But dear, do you wish to tell me that the warriors were influenced by you; a young girl, to annul the death sentence?"

"Yes, my dear Fritz," she replied; "that is what I assert. At that time I was not yet able to speak their language with perfect fluency. I threatened them that if they executed the terrible and unjust verdict, I would leave them. An Indian does not kill outright, he tortures to death. Caqua lives, of which you are convinced, and if I should determine this moment that he should die, he dies, I was then made Queen of the Chippewas and Caqua adores me. He looks after my wood and my horses and has made for me fine saddles. He is happy when he can do something for me. I furnish him with pipes and tobacco. His most dangerous foe on earth is whiskey. I sell his furs and buy traps for him. I do all I can for him with the exception of letting him get away from the village, for bad men will give him whiskey. See, Fritz, out of that monster I have made a lamb!"

"Birdie", Fritz exclaimed enthusiastically, "I am about prepared to believe myself that you are an emissary of the Great Spirit." So saying, he relapsed into his ancient weakness of drawing the dear creature to him and kissing her.

"Much that is written and spoken about the Indians is grossly exaggerated," she continued, "Much is wholly false. Americans take pleasure in sensational trash of that kind. In ordinary life the Indian is very simple. The terrible uprisings, in which the Indian will burn and murder unsparingly, are generally caused by the invidiousness and fraud perpetrated by white men upon their red brethren."

"What is the religion of your wild men?" Fichte asked Yellowbird, who replied: "The Indians are naturally superstitious. In all natural phenomena they look for a cause emanating from either a good or an evil spirit, i.e., from some mysterious, powerful being. Thunder and lightning are terrible occurrences to the Indian. Sickness is equally dreadful. The Indians rarely get sick. In case this happens, his fellows believe that an evil spirit has taken possession of him. Instead of being nursed, he is shunned. What is said of the Indians' praying, is nonsense. The Indian does not really know what prayer is. Those, who seek to instruct him in it, are generally frauds anxious to exploit him. I have caused many of these sorts of white hypocrites to be shipped beyond the confines of the village. The traditions of the Indians mostly rest on mere superstition. They have not the faintest idea of their origin. They explain the origin of the various tribes from the strife arising among the chiefs, the weaker of whom separated with their retinue from the rest and looked for other quarters until they felt themselves sufficiently strong to make war and defeat their enemies. The cruel extirpations of Indian tribes may be accounted for in that way. Our Solomon, for instance, well recollects that he belonged to a big tribe which roamed in the vast prairies where buffalo were in such plenty that the male members of his tribe devoted almost their entire attention to the hunting of that beast. He also knew that a portion of the Indians separated themselves from the tribe, that is, the weaker faction was driven to the north, or the winter, as they call it. He is also mindful of the fact that his tribe, the Chippewas, were always vanquished and decreased in numbers and were finally almost exterminated by the Menominee, another faction of a once powerful tribe."

"You cannot imagine, how deeply your narrative interests me," Fichte interposed; "I have read much in the old country about the Indians, but I am convinced that most of the stories on that topic are, as you have already said, untrue. How many chiefs are usually found in one tribe?"

Yellowbird answered: "Sometimes a few, sometimes many. If, for example, we today had but one chief and one of our tribe would distinguish himself tomorrow by some peculiar act of heroism, the chief would call a council. In case there were more than six chiefs in the tribe, the eldest of them would call a meeting at which the chiefs alone would participate. But if the number of chiefs was less, old warriors would be summoned instead. The deed of the candidate for admission for the chieftancy would be considered in all its bearings and finally a vote taken on the subject. If the vote turned out in favor of the candidate, a day is fixed, on which he is raised to the dignity of chief. Such events are celebrated in the most ridiculous fashion. Similar nonsensical ceremonies are current among whites on similar occasions. However, the Indians are far ahead of the deeply learned and civilized whites in that their chiefs must earn their own living and their dignity is not hereditary, but must be won. In our tribe we have no persons who, for pay, undertake to pilot our souls to heaven. Such drones are unknown among us. Our people are free men.[36] There is plenty of game in the white hunting grounds. They have no taxes to pay and are not subject to artificial training. Debts, worry about the daily bread and downcast spirits are unknown, and the highest position of dignity is that of a chief."

---

[36] Like many of the early settlers in Kiel, especially those who had fled the failed 1848 revolution in what is today Germany for America, author Henry Goeres seems to have been a "freethinker", one who held a dim view of organized religion. Colonel Henry F. Belitz, founder of Kiel, was also a noted freethinker.

X. THE QUEEN OF THE CHIPPEWAS.

"But, darling, are you not the Queen of the Chippewas? Fichte asked.

"This power," Yellowbird answered, "is one accorded to me by the chiefs of the tribe in consideration of the fact that after my reception into the tribe, fate willed it that the chase yielded better results than for a long time previous, there was a better harvest of corn, the rain set in at the proper season and very many male children saw the light of day."

The last remark Yellowbird accompanied with giving Fichte a slight push with her shoulder. She continued. "After I once seized the reins of power, I took care that there was no lack of happy accidents. For our wares we got ten times more than formerly. I kept them away from fire water. It is a matter of rare occurrence at the present day that one of our people falls a victim to his greatest enemy - liquor. Last year I succeeded in landing in the penitentiary at Wausau[37] a vendor of the vile stuff who repeatedly sold it to members of my tribe. For a similar offense another rumseller in that district had to pay a fine of five hundred dollars. Every month I look over the money in each one's possession. Even the chief has to obey my directions at that time. They must render to me an account of the way in which they spend their money. Spendthrifts are punished."

"Do you spank these also?" Fichte asked jestingly.

"No, Fritz," Yellowbird replied; "but I determine the number of blows they are to receive. The severest punishment which I can mete out to a member of my tribe is to exclude him from festivals and picnic excursions. We all have money and many more traps than formerly, as well as more corn, beans and potatoes, because I have insisted upon a rational method of agriculture and do not suffer needs to encroach upon the harvest. The squaws fancy themselves in heaven, because their burdens are lightened and they are protected from abuse. Once a year I travel to Milwaukee, the metropolis of the state, where I make the necessary purchases in reputable houses. None of the members of my tribe become the victims of scoundrels. In this manner I have driven the evil spirits out of our camp and am considered the paragon of virtue. Europe has not soldiers enough to force my Indians to plunge into the mad waters of the swollen river and there do hard labor for the preservation of the mill dam. You have seen yesterday how quickly and willingly they did so in accordance with my wish."

---

[37] This is likely meant to be a reference to the Wisconsin state penitentiary at Waupun (Waupun Correctional Institution), which has been in operation since the 1850s.

"Birdie!" exclaimed Fichte, rising and embracing Yellowbird; "Birdie! What have I not all witnessed yesterday! I have seen many great things, but the grandest and most sublime of all I have ever seen was when a lone, unpretentious girl, careless of fame or glory, appeared one a scene where raging torrents threatened to destroy a mill dam, on which the weal and woe not only of the proprietor, but also to some degree that of the settlers in the vicinity depended; where the property, in which a good family had planted its last hopes, was threatened with destruction by a mad flood. When none would or could dare the utmost, a noble being's voice, clear and pure and without terror, was head above the din. Drenched by the downpouring rain she sat motionless on her pony in the black, stormy night and half a dozen savages plunged with contempt of death into the surging element and all was saved."

While still holding Yellowbird in his arms, Fichte continued: "Birdie, my sweet Birdie, heaven itself has not seen anything below than when you on the night previous, without regard to anyone else, translated my directions to the savages, and how they carried them out, frequently wholly surrounded by water like reptiles and amphibia. Such a show, without training and rehearsals, earth had not yet seen! Birdie, my sweet Birdie, let me thank you again" and again he caressed her and covered her lips with glowing kisses, while tears streamed from his eyes. Seizing her chin with his right hand and pushing back her head so that it rested on his left arm, he gazed awhile into her lovely countenance and then said in a voice almost choking with emotion: "And this fair creature and great heroine is my bride!"

"And the commander-in-chief of the entire glory is my Fritz, my bridegroom," she shouted gleefully, escaped from his arms, stepped back a little and flew to him with open arms as if to crush him, exactly as Fichte had done towards her several times.

Fichte rested his head on Birdie's shoulder. For some moments they stood in silence, overcome by happiness and joy.

"Birdie", Fichte softly said at last; "your commander-in-chief of the whole glory must soon take his leave, for his time is expired and Birdie knows the value of order."

Mockingly, Yellowbird remained motionless in her old position. Neither did Fichte stir. Softly and jestingly Fichte repeated his admonition: "Birdie, your Fritz must go." Finally she raised her head and bent it back a little, then gazed earnestly and firmly into Fritz's face. A lovely smile, as sweet and inspiring as the beams of the rising sun on a spring morning, overspread her features, and ended with a clear, loud laugh. Breaking away from the arms of Fritz, she kept standing a few paces from him and told him while she was brushing back her hair: "Fritz, if you must go, I shall accompany you to the creek."

"Thank you, my darling!" Fichte replied; "will you permit me to get my walking stick which I felt in your wigwam?"

"We will go together, as I wish to put a wrap about my shoulders," she answered.

After the young people had gotten ready for the walk, they proceeded with locked arms. Hardly had they gone twenty paces when Fichte glanced back as if to take leave from the fairy castle. The wigwam behind Yellowbird's struck his gaze on account of its peculiar position and he asked: "Then the wigwam back of yours is uninhabited?" Yellowbird blushed and coughed a little and then said: "That wigwam is my pantry and woodshed and also serves as our village schoolhouse."

"In which you evidently act as the professor', he added jestingly.

"No Fritz," she said; "Caqua represents the professor. In the wigwam are assembled every morning my little ones, always neatly washed, dressed and combed, for otherwise they durst not appear before me. The exercises are opened with a few songs. In fine weather school is kept in the open air. I accompany the singing on the violin. I have been quite successful with the young savages I tell them of the pretty customs of civilized people and lay stress on the harmonious activity of the parents and how brothers and sisters think so much of each other. They will listen attentively and gaze up to me like a flock of doves. Then I speak to them on agricultural and horticultural topics and of the structure of the earth, its relation to the sun and moon, of the art of reading and writing, of railroads and factories, etc. Of course, I lecture in such a manner that the uncivilized little things can comprehend my meaning. I have paid considerable attention to the contempt exhibited by the boys and the girls and have succeeded in reducing it to a considerable degree. I am much vexed by the relapse in the case of Pona and Male, on whose behalf you have spoken. If you had my experience, you would certainly consider the punishment I have intended for her just and necessary."

"Excuse me, Birdie, your noble endeavor does not merit contradiction," he said; "I was sorry for the little one as she skulked away with a heavy heart after listening to your irrevocable verdict. You are not angry with me on that account, dear?"

Yellowbird gazed at him with a clarified look and said: "I respect you for it, for it betrays your good heart."

"Birdie," he said thoughtfully; "you are opposed to converting the Indians to Christianity. Wouldn't that civilize them?"

"What reasons have you for so thinking? Not civilization, but improvement is in question, and that is out of the question while their systematic exploitation is going on," she answered. "An army of regents and a thousand times greater one to defend them, as in your civilization, together with the hosts of lazy agents of heaven, for which the poor people of holy Christendom plague and toil, is certainly not worth imitating."

Fichte halted in admiration of Yellowbird and said: "Birdie, I am amazed at the extent of your knowledge. One might be tempted to believe that you were a pupil of one of our most radical revolutionaries of 1848, the mad year, in which my parents and I underwent so much suffering."

Yellowbird felt the blush rushing into her cheeks at the mention of the word revolutionaries. Fichte, however did not notice it, as the paint on her neck, hands and face effectually hid the blush. She painted as matter of precaution whenever she expected strangers or came in contact with others. Yellowbird continued as though she had not heard Fichte's remark: "As soon as the disproportion between the sexes has been rectified, the Indians will need neither civilization nor Christianity. Hence it is necessary that the women become independent in order to assume a more energetic air. Then they will have conquered! Physically I am not stronger than they are. The whole difference lies in my consciousness of possessing equal rights. However, my dear Fritz, since Christ is dead, Christianity has ceased to awaken this consciousness in any person. By and by I will relate to you some of my experience with Christianity in our camp. The last case I became cognizant of I will tell you at once."

The story of the evangelist, as related by Yellowbird, was as follows:

XI. THE EVANGELIST.

"One morning a Methodist evangelist, whose features betokened a desire to cover the whole earth with a shroud, entered our camp. He was accompanied by two sanctimonious looking brethren who made heroic efforts to imitate the facial contortions of their leader. As our village on the Wisconsin River is pitched on higher ground, I saw them coming from afar. The Indians whom they addressed said nothing, but simply pointed to my wigwam, at which the soul-saving delegation soon rapped for admittance. When I stepped out of the wigwam, attired like a queen, the minister at once inaugurated a sermon in such a solemn tone of voice that even our dogs got alarmed and frightened. His words were something like this: 'Go ye into the world and preach the Gospel, hath said a God, the sole source of salvation, a God who ruleth with his strong hand the sun, the moon and the stars. He is the sole and just God whom, pity 'tis, you poor savages, who have not yet been received into the grace of God, do not know.'

"The two fellows who accompanied him assumed a position like that of the two malefactors who were on the cross with Christ, and began to sob violently. The evangelist spoke further: 'As I have been told, you are the ruling spirit of these people who have not yet been received into the grace of God. It is said that you are thoroughly conversant with the language of the natives and are not devoid of education. Consider, oh esteemed Queen of these savages, that flesh is perishable, but that the life of promise is everlasting. The salvation of these your many subjects lies in your hands. Oh, oh, grant them a share in the eternal, heavenly glories! "Woe, woe!" saith the Lord to those who received his promise and heard it not! The sole God will banish such from his sight into the uttermost darkness, where there will be wailing and gnashing of teeth. Consider that you will be held responsible for all these souls, for you have received the enlightenment of God!'

"The two wretches accompanying him were almost dissolved in enlightenment and water. 'Who has sent you to me?' I very calmly asked the hypocrite."

"The sole and only God above us who has by virtue of his omnipotence created all that exists and without whose will no sparrow falls from the roof, no hair from our head, since he is omnipotent, omniscient and all just, was the solemn reply."

"According to your doctrine, then, he has created the Indians, too? I quizzed further."

"Yes, yes, my dear Queen, he has created all, all, he said."

"But, my dear sir, if he has created us, it is also his duty to look out for us," I said.

"Yes, yes, that he does, therefore he sends his servants who should spread his holy Gospel," he answered.

"Sir, your sole God could accomplish, by means of his omniscience and omnipotence, with a single wish that concerning which millions of you ilk, each in his own fashion and after his own opinion, have been attempting to accomplish for a long time past and which efforts have caused the spilling of much, very much innocent blood. But the same God says that only he that employs force will draw the kingdom of heaven towards him. We, however, sir, are no great friend of too many powers in this village. You probably know that we had rather do nothing at all and we justly make responsible him who has created us and who leads and guides us and without those will, as you say, no hair can drop from our head. The middle-men, however, who bargain off the mercy of this only God by the yard for money and chattels, we have invariably found to be liars, hypocrites and thieves. And therefore, begone!"

"The fellow made an attempt to say something, but I called Caqua and told him, in the native dialect, to make a sham attack on the trio and accompany it with such frightful howls and gestures as though he wished to tear them asunder with his teeth. Caqua was easily guided in his movement by my hand which I held to one side of my body. When I gave the signal of attack, that monster in times of peace broke forth from behind my wigwam with a howl like that of a hippopotamus. You ought to have seen the servants of the only God run. Their coat-tails were fluttering high in the air and Caqua with his unearthly yell was straight after them. All heated up from his mad chase; Caqua returned and pointed threateningly in the direction in which the allies of God had fled; 'Bird,' he said, 'Bird, no good white man,' and grinned with delight, which gave him the appearance of a gorilla. I could not help laughing and gave him my hand for the execution of my wish. Once upon a time, in order to express his devotion and affection, he squeezed my hand so violently that I uttered a cry. In order to avoid this, he placed my hand in his right hand and then his left hand over mine and thus shook it. Caqua does not know the limit of his power. Never did another soul-saver show himself in our camp."

Fichte was frequently convulsed with laughter during Yellowbird's recital, who mimicked as nearly as possible the actions of the gospel-sharks. He said: "No wonder they steered clear of your camp when the devil was sent in their pursuit."

Yellowbird and Fichte, by this time, had arrived at the creek, where they had agreed to take leave of each other for the time being. He placed his left arm about her shoulder and, kissing her, said: "Now, darling of my heart, farewell. In the course of a week we will probably see each other again. Perhaps you will need some trifles from the store. I am sorry that I cannot call on you again before Sunday, but the sawmill must be finished, for so many people are anxiously waiting for that event. When the sawmill is completed, settlers will come in droves."

"And spoil our fine hunting grounds," Yellowbird added.

"I will support you without hunting grounds, sweet girl," he answered; "of course, it grieves me to take you down from the throne of the Chippewas, but if you had desired to remain a queen, you ought not to have bestowed your heart on a Fritz Fichte. Parties from Chilton, Hayton and Sheboygan Falls have talked to me about having mills constructed in their towns, and offered me three dollar per day for my services. Don't you think that we can live on that and that there will be enough left over for you to play queen with? I will work as hard as I can to satisfy your wishes. Ah, Birdie he said, drawing her near him, "if you could but know what joy the consciousness that you will be mine some day instills me with? I dare not think of your impending trip to the Wisconsin River. And then you will be dead for me through the entire summer. But next spring you must be mine!"

"I will be thine, Fritz," she replied seriously; "for thus it is written in my heart, but please, Fritz, do not urge the wedding. As soon as I announce to you who and what I am, then lead me whithersoever you will, then I am thine. If possible, I will visit you during the course of the week. I do not expect you to preform the laborious journey to the camp after a hard day's work."

She offered him her lips - a signal that it was the last kiss, their farewell greeting for the day. Fritz rapidly disappeared in the dense forest and meditated on the doings of this eventful day as he hurried homeward over stumps and through fallen leaves. He had today ascertained more about his bride, although he was eager to learn what could have induced such a girl, pretty as a picture and endowed with an excellent education, to lead such a life. What might her secret be? He was no less amazed at her views of law and religion.

"It is strange", he thought; "her ideas are almost identical with those of my father, who was a fugitive revolutionary of 1848. If she had grown up among agitators and never heard any other views than theirs, surely not more could be expected of her in that line. What a splendid Sunday afternoon have I enjoyed and how much have I learned concerning the life and doings of the Indian girl. What Birdie says is undoubtedly true. How devoted she is to me! Coquetry is foreign to her. She acts according to her feelings and, with her tenderness, has never done any harm to anybody."

XII. KAAN.

When Yellowbird arrived at her wigwam, she found standing in front of it Kaan, who was not at all eager to meet his judge, as he knew that hope for mercy was vain. Much as he loved Yellowbird, she appeared very inopportunely to him, as he had a wholesome respect for a spanking. But he had to suffer it, for Yellowbird had so decreed and the dear queen could not do wrong. How near she had come!

"Ah", he thought; "had I but obeyed her orders! I could have finished the job in two hours, for Yellowbird does not ask anything unreasonable. She is good and just. I will never offend her again. Oh if I were but over it. The lash burns and Yellowbird applies it long and hard. Shall I make another effort to beg for mercy? Ah, Yellowbird is so good and so anxious that her children are the same."

Incredible as it may appear such thoughts floated through the lad's mind. He really felt profound remorse. None of the other children were allowed to be near when Yellowbird punished one of them, nor were they allowed to taunt the victims of her justice.

Yellowbird had approached in the meantime and told him with the mien of an angel: "Kaan, get the whip out of my wigwam." Kaan lost all hope of successfully suing for forgiveness. He obeyed and humbly handed his mistress the long and heavy twisted raw-hide. He stretched himself on the bench and without uttering a sound received a severe flogging from the soft hand of such a dear queen.

After this painful procedure, she told him in a tone as dispassionate as usual: "Kaan, tell the other children to attend school a little earlier tomorrow morning. Will you be obedient and diligent in the future? See, because you were lazy and disobedient, Pona also had to suffer. Because you were disobedient, your mother could not work for some time. Do you see the mischief a disobedient boy can do? I have punished you that you do not forget the wrong you have done. You know what you have to do tomorrow and I hope that henceforth you will be my dear, good boy. You may now look after the ponies."

Yellowbird entered her wigwam, and Kaan danced about like a lynx in the moonlight, because he was again to be Yellowbird's dear boy. Although he was still smarting under the spanking he had received, he had gotten over it and was again Yellowbird's dear boy. He ran into the woods to see whether any of the ponies had stuck fast in the swampy places.

In spring the bogs are the first to turn green. The poor ponies who have fed during the long dreary winter on nought save sprigs, feel a mighty longing for fresh grass and frequently penetrate far into a swamp. If they are not rescued in time, they perish, because on account of their miserable feed and the camping in the open on snow and ice they have become too weak to extricate themselves from the mire. It never grows as cold in the almost endless, dense forests as it does in the open country. It was Kaan's task to look after the ponies which, unless hunger urged them on, never wandered far away from the wigwams.

XIII. THE GIFT.

Mrs. Behl considered the veneration of her husband towards Yellowbird exaggerated, as Yellowbird, in her eyes, was nothing but an ordinary Indian whose only merit consisted in being possessed of an uncommonly pretty "mug" and who, consequently, was more revered by the Indians. In Mrs. Behl's opinion, Yellowbird's charms were the common property of the savages. A life such as that which Yellowbird undoubtedly was compelled to lead appeared to her as hair-raising, she durst not think of it; but that her husband discovered in such an uncivilized creature an iron will and an immense amount of almost divine qualities, seemed simply ridiculous - yes, insulting, to her. Of course, she could not blame her husband for being grateful to the girl for the service she had rendered him; yet he had thanked the Indians and, besides, paid them very well for their trouble. And how little stress was to be laid on the whole affair when one considered that time was of no value whatever to the lazy redmen! How blind her husband was! If it was inexplicable to Mrs. Behl that her husband classed Yellowbird among human beings endowed with sentiment and even character, it seemed to her abominable of Fichte, to have struck up a friendship with her and to converse with her, and she could not think of it without gall.

Mrs. Behl and Fichte were acquainted since childhood, their families having been neighbors. Fritz Fichte had received a good education and fulfilled the promise of his youth by developing into a very handsome man. He was nearly six feet in height, well proportioned, had blond hair and a smooth face. He was strong and skillful and a good mechanic. She always thought a good deal of "neighbor's Fritz". When her family emigrated and Fritz entered his apprenticeship with a shipbuilder, they were separated and gradually half forgot each other. When their parents settled down in the wilds of North America, she was sixteen and Fritz eighteen years of age. In those days, when a greater proportion of men than of women undertook the difficult and perilous wanderings into the immense virgin forest, girls were naturally much in demand.

Thus it came that Helene Schlicht, when scarcely seventeen years old, became the wife of Mr. Behl. Thanks to the domestic rearing by her mother, she proved a good housekeeper, although she had the weakness of boasting of her ancestry, a peculiar Germanic trait. In the old country her father had been a teacher at a high school and her mother a parson's daughter - and that was her pedigree. Mrs. Behl imagined that in wild America people such as hers could not be found, the Fichtes, who were also educated people, excepted, of course.

Mrs. Fichte had died of nostalgia some years ago. She was unable to accommodate herself to the new and poor circumstances in the wild country. Her husband lived along in his house, but was in daily intercourse with the Schlicht family who were his neighbors in the new as well as the old country. They proved a consolation to him, especially since the death of his wife. He spared no efforts to give his only child, Fritz Fichte, a higher education. The son was about to attend the University of Goettingen, when the fateful year 1848 changed the life programme of so many Germans very thoroughly and very rapidly.

Mrs. Behl was a comely, well-preserved woman of twenty-six years[38], and an excellent housewife, but in many respects very prejudiced. Her greatest weakness she displayed in her foolish pride of ancestry. She never otherwise spoke of her father than as a high school teacher and of her mother as a minister's daughter. In the old country, her husband had also been a teacher who, like the Schlichts, the Fichtes and many other families, were driven from German soil by the same fate.

Behl was much older than his wife. This may account for the fact that he almost worshipped her, although she was far beneath him in regard to education. It was rumored that Behl had left or had been compelled to leave behind in Germany a wife and children.[39] He entertained great schemes, he possessed considerable enterprise and he saw many castles floating in the air. He was the one who devised the trick regarding the plankroad. He had prospected for the water power in the depths of the forest. After convincing himself that the surrounding land was well adapted to agricultural purposes, he bought a large tract in the vicinity. Behl saw a great future before him. Under these conditions Kiel would not help booming. The sawmill was to begin operations in four weeks and the road to Sheboygan was to be completed by September. In the latter town many emigrants were daily arriving by boat. They would naturally follow the highway - which was the only one, a good one and owed its existence to him.

In his mind, Behl saw the forest felled, farms rising and Kiel peopled by ten thousand inhabitants within a decade.[40] Near the spot where the dam broke a few days ago, Behl had selected a site for a gristmill[41], for his residence, a gymnasium, factories, tanneries, etc. His greatest pleasure was to wander through the woods with his wife Helen and explain to her all his pretty projects.

---

[38] Mrs. Belitz was born in March of 1831; accordingly, she would have been 28 at the time of the story.

[39] Belitz was married previously in Germany.

[40] As of the year 2016, the population of the City of Kiel has yet to exceed 4,000

Mrs. Behl never entertained the slightest doubts concerning their execution. She invariable was in a high state of exaltation when returning home with her husband after such an aircastle-building trip. Mrs. Behl was fond of her neighbor's son Fritz Fichte, but she rather doubted whether he was such a consummate master in the projection of great cities as her husband was. Fichte was younger and handsomer than her husband, but not such a genius. Johanna, Schlicht's second daughter, was, by mutual consent of both families, regarded as Fichte's future wife, when Helen was married to Behl, for where in America could a lady be found the equal of her? This thought had struck deep roots in Mrs. Behl. That Fichte had started a liaison with a wild Indian, or at least an adventure, was a terrible blow to her. Mrs. Behl felt certain that Fichte had no idea of marrying the woman, but were not his actions in a manner insulting to such noble and educated people as themselves? Did he not publicly hug and kiss the savage maiden at the mill-dam? If she was Johanna, he durst not approach her henceforth. Indeed, he made no attempts in that direction. No one could find fault with Fichte. He toiled from early morn till late at night, never interfered with any one's affairs and disturbed and molested none.

At meals, Mrs. Behl frequently attempted to get Fichte to talk, but never succeeded, as she was by no means his equal intellectually.

Johanna Schlicht was but sixteen years old and had kept school in a log cabin during the winter. As her pupils numbered but eighteen and the school year embraced only three months, her salary as a teacher was necessarily small. Johanna was shorter, but smarter and prettier than her sister. She possessed a round, healthy face with regular features, light blue eyes and splendid hair which was almost white. For her age she was well-developed but strikingly pale. Although Johanna's education was no match for Yellowbird's, she possessed ordinary knowledge – sufficient to instruct the village youth. Mrs. Behl was proud of the fact that her sister was a teacher, especially since the latter could sing and play a little on the piano. The latter accomplishment, however, she found no opportunity to exhibit, as the howling wilderness was in those days devoid of pianos. What a difference between her sister and the savage!

Fichte's conduct was irritating to Mrs. Behl, but what was she to him? It was too much for the daughter of the high school teacher however that her husband was in the habit of paying such great attention to Yellowbird, who lived unprotected among totally depraved, beastly redskins, against whom she could impossibly have guarded herself. It was more than she could bear. She pestered her husband until he finally agreed to take her to the Indian village.

inhabitants.

[41] As mentioned earlier.

Under different circumstances the covering of a stretch of two miles along a narrow trail zigzagging through dark forest and dense underbrush would have dissuaded her from the enterprise, but the idea of triumphing over her husband by convincing him that Yellowbird was no better than she supposed, had such an irresistible charm for her that she never thought of the difficulties. Mrs. Behl being a conscientious housewife, she insisted on starting bright and early in order to be able to return before dinner, for she believed that without her supervision things at home would go wrong as her maid-servants were but children of the common race.

When Johanna heard her sister say that she was going to visit the Indian village, she insisted on accompanying her. There was nothing out of the way in that. Almost every settler even the women and children had visited the Indians. Besides, she had often expressed such a wish, even in Fichte's presence. She would have, indeed, been better pleased, if Fichte's sweetheart had not resided in that camp; but still she was determined to go, and since her sister and her brother-in-law went also, she could not imagine a better opportunity.

When Mrs. Behl had succeeded in finding a reliable woman, a laborer's wife, to take special care of her children during her absence there was no obstacle to the journey remaining. Mrs. Behl's children, two little girls, were evidently more precious beings then the children of ordinary mortals, their father being a – well, we know. At the proper occasions the father even rose to the rank of a professor.

"Well, children," Behl said at breakfast the following morning; "hurry up and get ready, for I must return soon to inspect the poor places in the new road which is nearing completion. On Thursday we will attempt to get that ironwork for the mill from Sheboygan. Since I sincerely wish you to have the pleasure of seeing the Indian village and as the Indians may decamp any day, I will cheerfully sacrifice the time needed for a visit thither, but not any more time than necessary. Therefore I must insist on your making haste."

"Henry," Mrs. Behl, who was garrulous, began in a tone of tragic pathos; "the main object of our trip is that you render to the Injun girl – what in the world is her name, anyway? Her she paused a moment until Johanna who held one of the children on her lap whispered to her "Yellowbird".

"Yes," Mrs. Behl continued, "Yellowbird, yellow bird; yellow snout (Gelbschnabel) would be more proper."

"What did you wish to say, Helen?" Mr. Behl impatiently interrupted her, "wherefore this wordy bombast?"

"What should be our main purpose but that you personally thank the yellow bird?" Mrs. Behl answered in an irritated manner, but rose to show her husband that she was preparing for the excursion.

"Helen! We have discussed this question in all its bearing. I am sorry that you who are otherwise of an excellent spirit have shown yourself so unjust, even spiteful, in a case in which we are under special obligations. You will, I hope, admit that I, who was attending to the work from the very beginning and closely observed everybody and everything, was in an almost desperate frame of mind. Our golden future, the existence of us all, depended on the preservation of the dam. I think I am in a position to know who is and who is not entitled to thanks. We certainly have no cause to complain of the settlers and the laborers, but when at the critical moment at the height of distress someone had to plunge into the rushing waters, none of them could be induced to dare it. Fichte alone could not do anything. The girl came to his aid; I have said these things over and over again. Why waste words about it? I am grieved that you are bent at all hazards to deny to the young girl the merit of her acts. The case might be different if she were a constant burden upon us and begged alms or undeserved fees of us, but I am sure, yes, understand me, Helen, I am firmly convinced that Yellowbird will never even refer to it. I say again that she is a noble child." While Behl was talking, he became very excited and indignant and tears streamed down his cheeks. The ladies did not venture to make any further remarks against the Indian girl, as Behl had spoken too earnestly and emphatically on her behalf.

In a few minutes, the women were ready to depart. In the meantime they had hatched out a plan which they laid before Behl as he returned from the gravel pit and was about to join them. Mrs. Behl addressed him in a very friendly tone as follows: "Henry, if you are under such great obligation to the girl, we ought not to be niggardly, but make her a handsome present. You would today certainly not be willing to lose our dam for thousands of dollars, and our future, which is closely dependent on it, for hundred of thousands."

"Come to the point, Helen, come to the point," Behl impatiently interrupted the impetuous course of his wife's eloquence.

"You ought to present the Injun girl with a decent gift," Mrs. Behl said in a loud voice.

"From the moment in which the girl distinguished herself, Helen," Behl calmly replied, "I had something of the kind in view. I have not been able to come to a conclusion regarding the nature of the gift. It was impossible to converse with you and Johanna on the subject; besides I would first have to pay a visit to town."

"Would you consider the presentation of a golden watch and chain extravagant, Henry?" his wife asked him.

"Yes, Helen, I would certainly take one with me today, if I had one," Behl replied.

"We have a watch that will answer the purpose, Henry," she said, "and if you will promise to replace it with a new one, Johanna is willing to part with hers. She does not need hers until the school term beings next fall."

"My word of honor on it," Behl said; "Johanna, before next fall you will have a new watch and one every bit as good as this one."

"But you must be the one to present it to her, Behl," Johanna said; it was the first time she addressed him this morning and added: "It would not look well for us to do so. It is your duty to present her with the gift."

"Let me have the watch, Johanna," Behl replied; "I will take charge of it."

Johanna brought the watch that rested in a plush-covered case. Her brother Hermann had recently presented it to her upon her becoming a teacher. It was an ordinary ladies watch with a fine chain which, according to the fashion of the time, was worn about the neck.

All preparations for the journey had now been made. When Behl hinted at the probability of Yellowbird's not accepting the gift, the women had to laugh very heartily. Mrs. Behl especially fell from one laughing fit into another. She exclaimed almost uninterruptedly: "Injun and not accept gifts! My lord husband, you are rid of the watch, as surely as I am standing in this room."

Behl was in the minority and allowed the peals of laughter to subside before quietly remarking that Yellowbird was entitled to the present and that he intended to hand it to her. Not one out of thousands of white women would refuse the gift and it would be but natural for Yellowbird to accept it.

After Mrs. Behl had given her final instructions to the servants and the women in charge of the children, they set out upon their trip. After the sawmill was passed, the company was compelled by the narrowness of the trail to march in single file. Fichte was wielding the hammer in the mill. Mrs. Behl could not resist wishing him, from a distance, a good morning and asking him snappishly whether care had to be taken not to bring home from the Indian village various kinds of vermin. You have frequently been there and perhaps had some experience in that line.

"That depends upon one's susceptibility to vermin, madam," Fichte replied in a somewhat irritated tone of voice; "I have frequently been in the village and have never yet been bothered by vermin."

Behl was pleased with Fichte's reply, greeted Fichte in a friendly manner and the party, with Behl at the head, moved on. Mrs. Behl regretted having addressed Fichte. She had fancied that nobody would have been able to make a reply to her witty remark, which was intended as a thrust at Fichte. His answer was a stinging rebuke to her. Johanna did not cast a glance at Fichte. He did not appear to exist for her. Behl took long strides and the women had hard work to keep up with him. They found the distance a very wearisome two-mile stretch, but made no complaint. They reached the brook and Behl saw first his wife and then her sister across. "We will soon arrive at our destination," Behl said.

But hark! What was that? They all held their breath and listened intensely. From a southeasterly direction, the singing of children, which seemed to emanate from the throats of angels, penetrated their ears.

"My God!" Behl said with great emotion; "one would be tempted to believe that he stood on the confines of paradise. It is a quartette. Such singing I have never before heard. It is faultless."

But hark! They all listened again.

"I have not deceived myself," Behl interrupted the silence after a while; "the singing is accompanied by someone on the violin and in a masterly manner."

Behl was a musician and very fond of his art. Among the few settlers in his district he had even started a singing society that was making considerable progress.

"I have never been so agreeably surprised in my life," Behl said. The women had forgotten all desire to mock, for the mystery of what was being conveyed to their ears made a powerful impression on them.

"Hurry up, children," he urged them on; "we must be near this paradise." They accelerated their steps and rapidly approached Yellowbird who was standing like a directress in the midst of her young pupils and accompanied her singing on her violin. She looked as splendid as on the preceding day and was arrayed in her best robes, as she intended to ride to New Holstein that day. New Holstein had been settled several years prior to Kiel by settlers who traveled via Fond du Lac. It boasted of a post office and some fine farms. Traffic was still difficult, however, and was carried on across Lake Winnebago and by team to Chilton and New Holstein.

Yellowbird's appearance was almost the same as on the previous day with the exception that she had put aside her pearl necklace. When Behl and his ladies drew nearer, they refused to give credence to the testimony of their eyes. Yellowbird was playing heavenly strains on the violin and her pupils were singing enchantingly. She stood among them like a fairy. The young people were so lost in the singing that their keen Indian eyes did not observe the approaching strangers.

Yellowbird having just previously turned her back, Behl and the two women were able to approach unnoticed close to the singers. Yellowbird and her little ones were a little surprised when they heard a lively applause at the close of the song they had been singing. When Yellowbird perceived the visitors, she took the violin and bow into her hand and greeted the newcomers in a measured but friendly manner.

"Miss Yellowbird," Behl addressed her, "when, while walking through the forest a few minutes ago, I heard the singing, I fancied myself approaching the confines of paradise. I never expected to find such singing here."

"Indians are very susceptible to music," Yellowbird answered; "as the little ones are amenable to guidance, it is not a difficult matter to teach them a few songs."

"But, Miss Yellowbird", Behl continued; "You have here a regular quartette, whose members sing with astonishing purity."

"We sing until all false notes are eliminated, Mr. Behl; we have plenty of time," she replied.

"Please do not be offended, Lady Yellowbird," he said; "I, too, play on the violin. As a teacher I have exerted myself to the utmost with my pupils, who are the children of civilized people, yet I have not been able to achieve such results with them."

"These children are very talented and particularly attentive," was Yellowbird's modest reply.

"But, miss, you do not say a word about yourself! How have you achieved such a mastery on such a difficult instrument? You easily change to any key and have the sweep of an artist," Behl observed.

Yellowbird burst out into laughter, clear, lovely, ringing. Every peal of her voice cut deep into Miss. Schlicht's soul. She felt that her cause was lost, that no man could resist such a being. Fichte the fresh, handsome, good, able man was lost to her.

"Mr. Behl," Yellowbird began to explain; "you must consider the I had to exercise their voices one by one, as I found them more or less adapted to this or that part, and after I had repeated the experiment dozens of times, why should not the music impress itself firmly upon me".

"I cannot play without notes, lady, although I am four times your age," Behl said. "You possess a mighty musical talent and must have had a great teacher. I am sure of that, because I have experience in that line. But for the very reason because you seem to wish to deceive mankind concerning yourself, and wrap yourself up in profound mystery, I will desist from asking any questions. I would, however, beseech you from the bottom of my heart to afford us once more the pleasure of hearing such heavenly singing."

When the arrival of the visitors interrupted the exercises, the children squatted Indian fashion on the floor. They did not appear to be at all curious, for a visit by white people was no novelty to them. Yet they had not for a long time seen such fair women. The younger one especially looked very beautiful. She wore her hair exactly as Yellowbird did, in a long and heavy queue hanging over her shoulder. But how pale she was and how pale her hair! Yet she was by no means as beautiful as their queen; for who could be as handsome as their dear, sweet queen! Some of the girls had placed their arm about Yellowbird's waist.

Pona and Kaan, the two rascals, gazed up so happily to their sovereign when she spoke and then again to the whites, as though wishing to say: "You have much, but a Yellowbird you have not."

Yellowbird lightly touched the violin with her bow and the little folks resumed their regular positions in the class with the speed of lightning.

Johanna was almost moved to tears by the touching picture presented by the little ones who looked up with such love to the girl with the violin. It was apparent to her that the girl had to be lovable, too, but Yellowbird was Johanna's rival – Yellowbird was passionately loved by the man whom she herself adored – and therefore she durst not admit anything in her rival's favor. She knew that Fichte was no hypocrite, as she had herself seen how he had hugged and kissed Yellowbird. Oh, if Yellowbird were but of a different cast!

When the little ones resumed their places and looked up as innocently and expectantly as a flock of chicks to their leader, Yellowbird gave the signal for the intonation of "Home, Sweet Home". They sang it so splendidly that Mr. Behl and the ladies were lost in rapture. Yellowbird, as before, accompanied on the violin and assisted with her voice whenever necessary. The latter was not often the case as her pupils were well-grounded. Although Yellowbird joined the singing but for moments at a time, her visitors could not fail noting how wonderfully clear and well-trained her voice was. Behl was overcome with emotion. Tears trickled down his cheeks and he involuntarily beat time.

At the close of the song Behl asked for the singing of another and explained to Yellowbird with what love he clung to singing and music. He and his ladies would feel very much honored by another song.

"I have never sung before visitors, Mr. Behl," said she; "and I must refuse today, but I will sing one with the children. They sang The Star Spangled Banner. Behl was delighted, especially with Yellowbird's voice. When the singing concluded, Behl extended his hand to the Indian girl, saying; "Miss, I cannot comprehend you!"

Yellowbird dismissed the children with the exception of Meeme and told them to return in the afternoon to resume the interrupted lesson. She then invited the company to step into her wigwam. The invitation was accepted immediately with thanks. Curiosity prompted the women and Behl was actuated by courtesy. Even Mrs. Behl found nothing to find fault with in the wigwam. Meeme was sent for fresh water and the mistress of the house prepared lemonade, cut up some lunch, procured two chairs from the mysterious wigwam and invited her guests to share her hospitality, which was accepted in the same manner and in the same spirit as the invitation to enter the wigwam.

Yellowbird's assortment of cake was not very large and about the same as that dished up to Fichte. Coffee was missing. If Fichte had been astonished at the rye bread the day before, the visitors of today were much more amazed. The women did not know what to say, Mrs. Behl had quite an elevated idea of her art of baking rye bread. She found that Yellowbird's bread was exactly like hers. If the Indian girl had been educated in Mrs. Behl's home and had worked for years in her kitchen, her rye bread could not have been any better.

"Carried away wholly by your singing, Miss Yellowbird," Behl started the conversation; "I must apologize for having forgotten to introduce the ladies".

"I have the honor to be acquainted with the ladies," Yellowbird said; "your wife and her sister, Miss Schlicht."

"How do you bake this fine cake, Yellowbird? I find it excellent," Mrs. Behl inquired.

Yellowbird volunteered the information asked and added: "The manner is very simple, isn't it, Mrs. Behl, and undoubtedly well known to you."

"Certainly I know how to bake the cake," Mrs. Behl answered; "but I did not think you could procure yeast out here."

"I often go to town, Mrs. Behl, once a year at least even to Milwaukee on business, and from the towns I bring with me all that I need in my kitchen. In this wigwam are to be found kitchen, lobby and bedroom," Yellowbird replied, laughing heartily.   Up to this time Johanna had clung to the hope that Fichte had to finally see that he could not found a home with a woman who strolled about all day long in woods and fields and possessed not the faintest idea of cooking and baking, but even this last hope was fast passing away. Yellowbird was apparently accomplished in all that he expected of her sex. Her robes were certainly her own handiwork although her style was Indian. Yet how accurate and tasteful they were. Miss Schlicht was devoured by morbid curiosity, yet she left the task of asking questions to Mrs. Behl who put the modest girl's patience to a severe test.

"How comes it, Yellowbird," Mrs. Behl inquired, "that such an excellent housekeeper as yourself is spending her time among these savages? You can make yourself very useful among civilized and respectable people."

Behl was angered at the common, almost vulgar remark of his wife and interrupted her by saying in a rather irritated tone of voice: "If Miss Yellowbird," he said, laying particular stress upon the world "Miss", to remind his wife that she had no right to call her merely "Yellowbird", "desired to utilize any of her accomplishments, she could do so most effectually with her splendid voice and good knowledge of music. People who can merely cook and bake are to be found everywhere in great plenty. It is the first accomplishment asked of a woman."

Yellowbird, however, was not satisfied with that declaration and said with the calm dignity of a GRANDE DAME: "Mrs. Behl, I owe the decent and civilized people nothing, I ask nothing of them and they have nothing to ask of me. The right to wander about where I please is my own as long as I do not molest others."

"Well said Miss Yellowbird," Behl replied; "for this right I sacrificed all my worldly possessions and had to flee from my home like a criminal. I am a political fugitive."

Yellowbird's eyes cast a lightning-like glance to where her other wigwam stood.

Behl tapped the fair girl on the shoulder and said: "Brave! Queen of the Indians! Brave! You are born for freedom and for a free country. If the rabble who permit themselves to be squeezed dry like a lemon year in and year out by the tyrants by the grace of God and the priests, would but once have a lucid moment and share your convictions, it would be better for mankind at large. Why should you be compelled to serve another against your will? For the preservation of the community. Yes! But, as it is, the laborers must support all, and those who prescribe the mode of support are drones and swindlers. This country will share the fate of other countries."

"How long," asked Yellowbird, "before these fine forests will be no more."

"You are right," Behl replied; "I myself have gazed with supreme delight at the pine and tamarack giants in these woods, and calculated what money I would gain with my saw-mill after it had sawed the giants of the forest into boards."

"And thus will it ever be," Yellowbird said. "The one drives away the other. We Indians, who until a short time ago owned all this vast territory, and who roamed about really free, without knowledge of mortgages and taxes, are driven back further and further. Yes, the day is not very far distant when the Indians will have wholly disappeared from the face of the earth. They will owe this solely to the civilized and intelligent white."

"But, Miss Yellowbird," Miss Schlicht interposed for the first time; "the buffalo and deer and all the other fine animals inhabited this country prior to the Indian. They too will soon have disappeared and that will have to be laid solely at the door of the uncivilized and disrespectable Indians who lived without knowing mortgages or taxes."

"Those animals would never have been exterminated by the Indians, my dear miss," Yellowbird promptly answered; "solely for their hides the buffalos are butchered by the thousand by the whites. The Indian will kill no more game than he needs for his support. The fine meat of the buffalo rots on the vast prairies. This species would never have been wholly exterminated by the Indian."

"According to your theory," Miss Schlicht quickly added, "all right is founded upon might. If the Indians had known their own strength, they could easily have strangled all invaders."

Yellowbird parried this charge as follows: "It was certainly not the Indian's fault that such was not done. The whites proved to be more cunning than the Indians. But why should people starve in the old county, when there is plenty of subsistence for many millions in this country? Of course, the Indians did not concern themselves with this question, as they are anything by philanthropists. Nobody knows whence they came nor how long they have been in possession of this country. I presume that nature produced them here as she produced negroes in Africa and whites in Asia and Europe. This land, together with the buffalo, the deer and other game, decidedly belonged to them."

"You are right, Miss Yellowbird," Behl said. "The Indians were on many occasions defrauded of their land, yet the government has allotted large reservation to them."

"Yes, Mr. Behl," she replied; "the government treats the Indians exactly as the fowler treats birds. He cages the birds as soon as they are caught. Yet, if the bird had to choose between the cage and the free air of heaven, even though the former should be of massive gold, if would undoubtedly prefer to live in the open air."

Behl admitted this unreservedly and said: "That is also true, dear miss; but I now propose that we drop this theme. It leads to nothing and I fear that you will soon have vanquished all of us. I must repeat, esteemed Queen of the Chippewas, that I cannot comprehend you on the field of general knowledge also. You are a great riddle to me."

"And I, Miss Yellowbird," Mrs. Behl added, "must openly confess that I cannot get over your pumpernickel. I am also astonished at your other cake and the lemonade."

"Would you not also like to know how she prepared the lemonade?" Behl laughingly asked his spouse, in order to cut off a volley of questions that she was likely to fire at Yellowbird. "You are perhaps very busy today and our curiosity robs you of time."

"Your call is very agreeable to me, Mr. Behl," Yellowbird replied; "I have nothing to do today except to ride over to New Holstein to get the mail."

"You are in correspondence then?" Behl inquired.

"I merely would like to get a newspaper to ascertain the current market prices of pelts and furs," was her answer, "if possible, we will sell our supply of these articles before we break camp for our trip to the Wisconsin River. We would thus save ourselves their cumbersome transportation."

"Where do you generally market them?" Behl inquired.

"Mostly in Milwaukee," Yellowbird replied quickly, for Mrs. Behl was balancing a host of questions on her tongue, "with about twenty ponies we bring them in one day via Calumet to Fond du Lac, from there we take the train to Milwaukee. The next day we return by train from Milwaukee to Fond du Lac. Solomon, our chief, and myself attend to all the buying as well as selling. Two young Indians remain outside of the city of Fond du Lac and camp in a tent, while our horses are grazing. They meet us at the depot, whither they also brought the good with the ponies, upon our return, and in about eight hours we are home again."

"But, miss," Mrs. Behl, who could restrain herself no longer, said; "I do not believe that a white girl who lays any claim to propriety would travel through night and mist alone with three Indians."

"Mrs. Behl," Yellowbird replied in her calm manner, "I fear a hundred thousand Indians less than one white tongue; for the former harm me less than the latter."

"If any one can know this, it must be yourself, Queen," Behl interjected rapidly; "for you have intercourse with both."

Behl then continued: "I will now explain the reason for our presence here. We came here to express to you in common our most cordial thanks for the unselfish services which you have rendered us in a moment of great distress, and at the same time to offer you as an acknowledgement and memento of our thanks a present consisting of a golden watch and chain."

Yellowbird began to laugh loudly. Behl had produced the casket containing the watch and chain and stool like a servant of the Lord before the Queen of the Chippewas, who continued to indulge in her hearty laughter. Behl and his two companions gazed at each other and did not know how to act.

"The watch is Miss Schlicht's," Yellowbird exclaimed, still laughing and pointed with her finger to the center of the golden case, in which the words "J. Schlicht" were engraved in very small but legible letters. Mr. Behl, the only one of the trio who was sincere, also began to laugh. He and Yellowbird appeared to be vying with each other in hilarity.

"Yes dear miss," he said at length; "such is the case. I had intended to buy another watch like this for my sister-in-law, as soon as the highway is completed and traveling to town less of a hardship; but I did not wish to keep you waiting that long."

"I could have stood the waiting very well," Yellowbird replied; "and I pledge you my word that I will cheerfully wait until the Sheboygan River has been made navigable from here to where it empties into Lake Michigan[42]. I cannot accept your gift, no matter how good and noble your motives may be. Our clock is the great, dear sun. Whether it shines in a clear sky or is enveloped in clouds, our eye sees it fully as distinctly as I have read the name of the watch, Mr. Behl. But in order to be just, let me tell you that neither you nor any member of your family are under the slightest obligation to me. What I did, I did merely out of love to Mr. Fichte, who is now my betrothed. I have already received his thanks which consisted not in a watch and chain, but in his acknowledgement and a hearty kiss; which is by far more valuable than silver and gold."

---

[42] I.e., until the end of time.

XIV. THE TELLTALE NOTE.

This frank but entirely unexpected confession of the fair Indian destroyed the entire supply of bombs which Johanna had gathered to throw at the hated girl at an opportune moment. She had long since allowed her sister, Mrs. Behl, to inspect her array of explosives and had rehearsed their discharge in all possible variations. Her strongest missile consisted in the following reproach: Egoism, pure egoism inspired your actions, all to gain Fritz Fichte. It was all the same to you whether the good man, who was accustomed to an orderly and moral life, would suffer decadence at the side of a savage or an adventuress.

Miss Schlicht was, indeed, in the proper mood to give vent to her hatred. The annihilating affair with the watch had done the rest. Yellowbird, however, had called her to a halt and checkmated her. The Indian girl was far different from what Miss Schlicht had imagined her to be. She stood before her as a highly educated, handsome and noble woman, whom her own brother-in-law likened to an artiste. Miss Schlicht was frequently praised on account of her voice and she herself entertained a high opinion of it, but was her singing compared to Yellowbird's? In spite of her youth, Miss Schlicht had an aversion to all exaggeration. Novels, in which the hero or heroine are endowed by the author with supernatural qualities, were repulsive to her. Yet here she stood in the very presence of an almost supernatural being, not on the stage of a metropolitan city, shining in splendor and luxury no, in an Indian camp in the midst of a primeval North American forest, and this creature was the bride of a young man to whom she felt attracted by an intense love.

Who could she be, this Indian girl? The more one attempted to annihilate her, the more she shone as a heroine and stepped into the foreground. Whence did she come and how did she manage to get that education? Johanna tortured her brain in vain, while her heart threated to burst.

Mr. Behl had again put the fateful casket into his pocket. He was in a triumphant mood. He would, of course, have been much pleased, if he could have caused the girl some pleasure with the watch, as a reward for her noble act, which was the more esteemed by him the more Yellowbird exerted herself to belittle it. He thought of his victory over the women and was resolved to taunt them some day with the excessive laughter and derision they had showered upon him when he hinted at the possibility of Yellowbird's not accepting the present.

"Children! It is time for us to return," Behl said to the women, and then turning to Yellowbird: "We would like to linger here longer, for in your presence one becomes oblivious of space and time, but we are seriously compelled to think of returning. Since you will under no circumstances accept a present from me, I will at least once more express to you my most heartfelt thanks. I would like to ask you, how you or the Indians learned the entirely practical use of the reed sacks which proved so very efficient in preventing the destruction of my dam."

"The Indian is very practical," Yellowbird replied, "As he is dependent upon himself in all things, his faculties are rapidly developed in certain lines. I have often observed, how the Indians fill traveling bags with earth and use them to dam up small streams and creeks, so that but a small aperture is left for the water to flow through. In this aperture boxes made of laths are placed so that all fish must pass into them. When I heard the first alarm signal, I had not yet retired, and as my favorite pony was accidentally feeding on salt close to my wigwam, I had no difficulty in arriving first upon the scene, as our horses, like children of nature, find their way as safely in a pitch-dark night as in broad daylight. When I saw Fichte's desperate strait and that the mill-dam could hardly be saved from destruction with the means at his disposal, I immediately thought of the process of which I have just spoken. A moment latter I was back in our camp. From afar I gave the alarm, consisting in a certain cry, and the preparations which, as you see, were executed, were at once made; for you can depend upon an Indian's word. However, Mr. Behl, if you wish to do me a great favor, please do not mention the affair again. You know my motives. I expect you as a gentlemen, to do so."

"Miss Yellowbird, you are noble," Behl replied; "I would like to make you another offer which, in case you accept it, will cause me and all the settlers in this vicinity great pleasure. Miss Yellowbird, summer is approaching. Let us celebrate together one day in the country. If you will sing a few songs with us, it will be a feast such as has never before been witnessed in a virgin forest. I have founded a singing society which meets twice a week. Please, Miss Yellowbird all New Holstein will celebrate with us."

Behl had seized Yellowbird's hand and was earnestly beseeching her to grant his request. She said: "Mr. Behl, our departure is near at hand. Our spring journey is due. Besides, I could never make up my mind to partake in festivities, in which my poor savages had no share."

Mr. Behl's eyes glistened with delight, for he fancied he had gained his object. "Bring them all with you," he said; "sing a few songs with the children. You and they will be admired and take all hearts by storm."

"My little ones must and durst not be admired," she replied seriously; "it is the most dangerous thing in the world for anybody especially young people. As soon as my pupils notice that they are being admired, that they begin to entertain a feeling then that they are doing better than other children, then their singing will no longer be as fine, as pure, as sweet, because they fancy then that they are on the high road of becoming artists."

"In my house you will be cordially welcome," Behl continued, who did not give up all hope and was something of a crank on the subject of singing and music.

"Mr. Behl, I promise you nothing, but I shall under no circumstances participate in you projected festival," she said.

Mrs. Behl, who was painfully affected by the subservient part played by her husband before the "Injun" girl, could not restrain herself from remarking: "You run no risk, Yellowbird, my pardon, Miss Yellowbird, in entering our home. Today it is still a mere shanty, but next year we will inhabit a palace. It is no disgrace for you. We are of a good descent. Our father was a high school teacher and our mother a minister's daughter. My sister, Miss Schlicht, is a schoolteacher. You can safely risk paying us a visit. If the Revolution (at the sound of this word Yellowbird's eyes wandered fearfully to the adjacent wigwam) had not broken out in Germany in 1848, we would certainly not he here. In Germany we were respected people. My father even was an alderman. We never thought and had no need of thinking of the possibility of ever living out here among uneducated people."

At the conclusion of her oration, Mrs. Behl wiped the perspiration from her brow, for she had exerted herself mightily.

Miss Schlicht sought to add weight to her sister's words by adding: "I too, Miss Yellowbird, am of the opinion that you would incur no disgrace, even though you be a queen, as you are called in jest, of these people who, strictly speaking, are below the level of a beast, that is, in respect to savagery and cruelty."

Yellowbird replied in a very serious tone: "I do not understand, ladies, what right you have to speak of degradation. What the savage cruelty of my comrades, of which you speak, Miss Schlicht, is concerned, you as a teacher ought to know that their bloodiest transactions, in comparison with the butcheries inaugurated by white rulers, are mere nose-bleedings. Just think of Ivan the Terrible, of the Roman wholesale assassins Tiberius, Caligula and Nero; just think of the barbarous wars in which entire nations were annihilated; think of the Crusades, of St. Bartholmeous Night[43], of the Inquisition and thousand of other terrors begotten by a lofty civilization. Look at the southern portion of our country and see how in our neighboring states slavery, trading in human flesh and maltreatment of human being is in flower; and at the indications what the disgrace will soon spread over the entire country. These are the products of a lofty civilization and of Christianity. Our Indian is cruel only to his foes who scalp him if they get him, in their clutches.

"Revenge is sweet as a proverb is clothed in fine language, but our savages apply it literally. This is the difference between the wild Indian and the civilized white Christian. If you are a teacher, though you may teach only the elementary branches, you ought to know all that."

Yellowbird spoke with her customary calmness. The two daughters of the high school teacher felt as their brother once did, that they could not begin to cope with the girl. They were inclining toward the belief that they were confronting an emissary of hell, sweet as sugar externally.

Behl was very much delighted with the discomfiture of his companions. He was a very liberal and just man. (He knew that his wife and her sister made every effort to triumph over the Indian girl, who in an effective yet gentle manner brought their efforts to nought). Whence did she come? As an educated man, he knew the toil and cost of acquiring knowledge, especially in music. How long did many teachers not labor with him until he could accomplish anything in that line? But how did this girl manage to make so much headway among Indians?

Behl had made up his mind to call on the mysterious Indian maiden in his capacity as a musician. He intended to let their musical accomplishments be the instrumentality of bringing about a perfectly harmless goodfellowship. He felt pretty certain of gaining his point. People from far and near came to him for advice, even in legal matters. He had some experience in legal affairs, especially in matters of property rights, He was not an attorney at law, but nevertheless a kind of second Moses in the Desert. He was not wanting in energy and perseverance.

---

[43] 1572 massacre of French Protestant Huguenots by Catholics on the feast of St. Bartholomew

Inspired with this aim in view, he took leave of Yellowbird, thanked her politely for her hospitality and walked away after informing his companions that while he paid a short visit to the Indians they should make ready for the homeward journey. With a friendly bow to Yellowbird he left the wigwam.

Before the women took their leave, Mrs. Behl addressed Yellowbird again, saying: "I regret to be compelled to mention something which I had rather pass over; but since the matter concerns the honor of my sister and she is under my care, I cannot be silent. Yesterday I visited my brother and while conversing with him about the break in the dam naturally came to speak about yourself. He then told me a story about a plumb line. I know not what a plumb line is, as I never converse with laborers or artisans; but whatever that may be, according to your remarks my sister Johanna would be a thief. My brother is ill at present, but as soon as he has recovered, he will affirm what I had said. Now it is not, Miss Yellowbird? Do you really suspect my sister of having stolen the plumbline?"

"I do indeed strongly suspect your sister of having smuggled it into the hunting pouch of an Indian; yes, madam," Yellowbird replied.

Johanna was weeping, but since her sister had the floor, she did not care, nor durst say anything. She knew her sister in that direction.

"Was not the plumb line Mr. Fichte's property?" Mrs. Behl asked.

"Yes," was Yellowbird's reply.

Mrs. Behl continued: "Now I ask you to give the reasons that lead you to your conclusion. Sensible reasons, of course. I also ask you, Miss Yellowbird, always to bear in mind and never to lose out of sight our descent."

Yellowbird made no attempt to interrupt Mrs. Behl's wordy effusion; but, when the latter paused, she repeated that she suspected Miss Schlicht for the reason already stated and that she could not disabuse herself of the suspicion until she herself had designated it as false.

Miss Schlicht exclaimed: "You certainly seem to assume, Miss Yellowbird, that I was actuated by the motive of hurling a firebrand between you and Fichte! I hope you do not consider me capable of such baseness."

"Yes," Yellowbird replied; "you have expressed the motive for the deed and I consider you capable of having, for the reason stated, acted thus. I am forced to this conclusion, since Caqua told me so. He had nothing to do with anyone else and what he tells me I consider as true as the gospel."

"Is Caqua the Indian who stole from the day-laborers who had never done him an injury, their tools, and suffered the inhuman punishment in consequence?" Johanna asked with mocking bitterness.

"Yes, Miss Schlicht, he is the identical individual," was the reply.

"Then I cannot understand how you can be so sure of your ground. Caqua is a thief," Miss Schlicht said.

"Caqua is a man of honor, Miss Schlicht," Yellowbird replied; "I will pledge my word upon that, but before we take up Caqua, you had better explain. Until now you have not yet definitely declared that you did not put the plumb line in question into Caqua's hunting pouch while you sister was paying him for some game he had delivered?"

Instead of answering the question, Johanna asked: "What is the use of my answering, since, according to your conviction, I am beneath your savages as far as credibility is concerned?"

Yellowbird replied: "My pupils must answer my question directly, miss, or be prepared to receive their punishment. As I have no right to treat you as my pupils, I move that we abandon this topic."

Mrs. Behl said in a questioning tone: "My God! How is it possible that two ladies can engage in a war of word about a mere bagatelle, a cord costing probably a few pennies?"

"Caqua had to suffer inhuman punishment, because he stole, your sister remarked a moment ago," Yellowbird replied; "he committed the deed not for plunder but out of revenge, I am sure of that. Yet he was punished. If he had stolen the plumb line, I would have punished him in addition. It is immaterial to me whether the cord is worth cents or dollars. Theft is theft." "Helen, it seems almost as though we stood before the judgment-seat of God," Miss Schlicht said to her sister; "let us depart. The stern judge, the Queen of the "Injun", might otherwise sentence us to be scalped!"

Even this remark was insufficient to satisfy Johanna's sister who, in spite of all her prejudices, began to feel ashamed in the presence of the young Indian girl. She desired to bring the conversation to a close, but could not refrain from remarking that Johanna had never put herself to any trouble on Fichte's account. "Of that I can assure you," Mrs. Behl said; "but you certainly will not demand that she shall confess to you."

"I demand nothing, madam, not even your opinion," was Yellowbird's reply, "My judgment is fixed. Your sister played the trick for no other purpose then to cast suspicion upon us. The idea was that Mr. Fichte should miss the plumb line and hunt for it until it finally bobbed up in our camp, to impress him that his bride, or beloved one, or at least her tribe intentionally robbed him."

"I have not put the plumb line into Caqua's hunting pouch," Johanna flared up. She was driven to this definite declaration by Yellowbird's calmness and logic.

"Then you have not written this note either, miss," Yellowbird said to the school ma'am, whose innocence was attached, while producing from her leather belt a small scrap of paper. The pale girl colored and Mrs. Behl also blushed, when she perceived her embarrassment. Yellowbird with her usual calmness unfolded the paper and held it up to Johanna's eyes. It contained a few words like "yellow beak", "yellow bird" and other meaningless mockeries. A painful silence ensued.

"Have you written the note, Miss Schlicht?" Yellowbird asked; "you will surely not claim that Caqua did."

"No," Johanna cried out, while her breast was heaving violently.

"This scrap," Yellowbird continued, "was fastened, to the cord with a needle. I have not shown it to Fichte out of regard for his feelings. The note evidently failed to reach its destination. The person from whom it emanated presumed that the Indian girl would give it to him for whom it was intended. I have not even spoken to Fichte about it. Miss Schlicht, you have told the truth. You have not written the note. I ascertained the writer, however. It was a boy by the name of Kleinschmidt[44] who could not find the way to New Holstein. He informed me that upon the request of his teacher, Johanna Schlicht, he had copied the words as he found them written on a slate which she handed to him. I told the youth that I found the note, where upon he gave me an explanation without entertaining any thought as to its significance. The lad appeared to be innocent and perhaps will remain so, thanks to the excellent training he is receiving in school. Now, in order to prove to you, ladies, that I wholly appreciate your station in life to which you can look up both from the paternal and maternal side, I promise that I will accept your invitation and on a day to be determined by you, upon the condition that you, Miss Schlicht, assert before Kleinschmidt, who will work for Mr. Behl, until school opens, that he had lied.

"Give me the note, Miss Yellowbird, I will take the fellow to task, I too can be severe," Mrs. Behl said in the capacity of a mediator.

"No, madam, the boy has enough to put up with at school and too much is unhealthy," Yellowbird said.

"Excuse me, miss, I have rapped several times, but no one in the wigwam seems to have heard. I heard so much from on the outside. I am convinced that you had to explain the minutest details of your cooking and baking and write out the prescriptions for your pumpernickel and lemonade," said Behl who was anxious to start for home.

---

[44] A brother of Mrs. Belitz and Johanna, one Gerhard Schlichting from the Town of Herman, married Adeleid Kleinschmidt. A young Kleinschmidt also passes news of the dam rescue in Kiel to the Johanna and Mrs. Belitz's parents in Sheboygan Falls. So it may be that this indicates Kleinschmidt was a relative of Johanna – further reinforcing the idea of collusion or trickery.

"I do not like to write, Mr. Behl," Yellowbird answered with such a naive, childlike and fascinating smile, as though not a harsh word had been uttered.

"But now, good bye, dear miss; have you not yet been able to make up your mind to visit us?" With these words Behl extended his hand to Yellowbird.

"That depends very much on the weather and your ladies, Mr. Behl," was her answer. Letting go of her hand Behl said: "You look out for fine weather, miss; I will look out for the ladies."

The visitors took their leave. Johanna thanked Yellowbird for the entertainment and then tripped into the open. She felt miserably. Mrs Behl cordially shook Yellowbird's hand and remarked that all would turn out well in the end. Behl marched in the van. He could not find word to express the surprises he had experienced today. The girl must come of a good family, he thought, and be in close touch with a great master of music. He evidently was thinking of the settlers of New Holstein, many of whom were political fugitives and educated men, with whom he was in frequent intercourse. Among all of them, however, he did not find one who was a match for Yellowbird. He was too good a musician not to be sure of that. Nevertheless he believed it possible to find out what master had been her instructor on the violin and what teacher imparted to her so much knowledge. Behl was a good hand at asking questions. His wife was also proficient in that line. He was however, many times more cunning than she. Yellowbird had not made as good an impression on the women as on him. He became aware of that very quickly. He also noticed that Johanna had wept. "What is the matter with Johanna?" he asked his wife, while looking at a lofty tamarack.

"Johanna is not feeling well," Mrs. Behl replied; "I think the unpleasant Indian odor had an evil effect upon her nervous system. Johanna is tender and very sensitive."

"But Helen! How can you be so cruel to a sister?" Behl said; "was Yellowbird's wigwam not as clean and fresh as the girl herself? I wandered throughout the entire camp and did not know what to say. There was a clothesline with wash back of every wigwam, of course, not at much as among many of the whites. Yet I am convinced that their wash is fully as well taken care of as that of the average of laborer's families."

"But, Behl, since when do you occupy yourself with wash?" his wife asked him laughingly.

"Do not misunderstand me, Helen," Behl replied; "I do not busy myself about your wash. But when you bear in mind what views we generally entertained about the wash of the Indians, do you not find such progress among the savages very surprising. I must frankly confess, wife, that today I experienced something of which I had never dreamed, never could have had the faintest suspicion. Have you not amused yourselves or do you envy Yellowbird on account of her pumpernickel?"

"I am now thinking of the children and Johanna. The Indian girl and her pumpernickel are very remote from my mind," Mrs. Behl said briefly.

Behl knew his wife's weakness. He observed silence and gazed at the slender hemlocks that reared their lofty crests into the sky. He made up his mind, that if he traversed this path again, he would do so alone.

XV. JACK SHEPARD.

While Yellowbird and Meeme were busy peeling potatoes, Kaan returned with a mess of fish and some watercress which is found in great abundance in the streams and springs of Wisconsin. He was standing behind Yellowbird and playing with her queue that extended halfway down her back. Yellowbird knew exactly what the lad was waiting for: he had not yet received a word of thanks from her. He was overjoyed if she but laid her arm on his shoulders and pressed him tightly to her. After the potatoes were peeled, Yellowbird turned to Kaan and said: "You appear to have been up early this morning. Have you caught the fish in a lake or in the river?"

"In Cedar Lake," Kaan replied in a happy frame of mind and asked: "Do you know that lake?"

"Certainly I know it," she replied; "we come past it when we ride to Fond du Lac. It is a wonderfully pretty little lake[45]. You have made a considerable trip this morning."

Kaan answered: "Pona and I were at the lake at sunrise. We speared at the outlet of the lake as many fish as the ponies could carry."

Yellowbird put her arms around the lad and invited him to dine with her and Meeme today. She told him to get Robin, her pony, and explained to him that on account of the visitors she received in the morning she had been compelled to postpone her intended trip to New Holstein until the afternoon and that therefore they would dine earlier than usual. She promised Kaan he would be allowed to accompany her which filled the lad with intense joy.

---

[45] Which lake is this? It does not appear to be what is today known as Cedar Lake in the Town of Schleswig (which did bear the name of Cedar Lake at least as early as 1878 according to a map from that year). Note that Yellowbird suggests a "Cedar Lake", but Kaan then asks if she is aware of it – and she implies it is a considerable way from the camp. While cedar-lined lakes are common in the area today (Shoe Lake, Graf Lake, Elkhart Lake, etc.) and likely were at the time, given that it is a "wonderfully pretty little lake", this could be what is today known as Crystal Lake, just south of Elkhart Lake, as it was referenced as "Cedar or Crystal Lake" in *The Physical Geography of Wisconsin* from 1916 and would be en route to Fond du Lac if one headed due south from Kiel before turning west toward Fond du Lac....but Yellowbird earlier says that their usual route to Fond du Lac was "via Calumet", which would seemingly not use such a southerly route – only Wolf Lake near Mt. Calvary comes to mind if a somewhat indirect route were taken. Still, in the final chapter of this book, the narrator notes that Yellowbird's pupils fished in Elkhart Lake, and Elkhart Lake, lined with cedars, does have a defined outlet that may align with Caqua's report.

Kaan shot out of the wigwam like a madman and acted in the wood like a delirious squirrel, for the sweet, dear Yellowbird had today made him exceedingly happy.

Yellowbird drew from her bosom a pretty little ladies watch of rare make and set with sparkling gems.

"It is now half past ten," she muttered to herself; "at half past eleven we can be off and by six o'clock we can be home again." The man she wished to visit lived two miles beyond New Holstein.

Meeme started the fire and Yellowbird prepared the noonday repast which consisted of potatoes, lettuce, baked fish and cold game. She always had a plentiful supply of game and fish, with which the forests and streams abounded in those days. The hunting grounds of the Chippewas were extensive and rarely entered by white sportsmen. They dined in the mysterious wigwam, to which Meeme brought the table from Yellowbird's wigwam. Meeme was Yellowbird's constant attendant. Cuquin (meaning "Leapfrog") the Indian girl who had been wounded in the ear by her brother, had not yet received her punishment. She was doomed to get her spanking, the time for which had been fixed by Yellowbird for the following evening. Cuquin was doomed to feel the rod and neither prayer nor entreaties could ward off the chastisement. The offenders were not permitted to approach their queen until after they had received the punishment decreed them. Kaan was approaching whistling and singing. He rode Robin and all the other ponies followed. He gave the animals salt and saddled Robin. Kaan admired Yellowbird's saddle, the handwork of Caqua. It was adorned with a fox and a bear head.

Kaan and Meeme ate with knife and fork and behaved at table with as much propriety as the best trained children of whites.

At noon, Yellowbird and Kaan started. They were picturesque looking. Yellowbird wore a light-colored dress and a blanket thrown loosely over her shoulders. Kaan had been permitted to put himself into fine array, but not quite to the full extent of his taste, for that would have displeased Yellowbird.

Yellowbird was in a happy mood. She got possession of two newspapers, the New York Staatszeitung[46] and the Milwaukee Banner and Volksfreund[47]. She succeeded in purchasing a bushel of potatoes of which she had run short and some bran for the pumpernickel. In view of her impending journey with her tribe to the Wisconsin River, she did not make large purchases. Kaan loaded the merchandise secured into the sacks attached to the sides of his pony.

---

[46] A prominent U.S. German-language newspaper published since 1834. It was decidedly in favor of the failed 1848 Revolutions in Europe (as its editor and a key staffer were involved in the agitations). As will become clear in the story, many of

Yellowbird missed the main object of her trip, however. Her confidential adviser was not at home. He had left in the morning for Chilton, the county seat of Calumet County. She was well-acquainted with his wife who thought very highly of her. The two women, however, never spoke among each other of business Yellowbird had to transact with the other woman's husband.

Mrs. Gruen showed Yellowbird around her garden, which she had put into fine shape. Kaan had removed the bits from the horses and allowed them to graze. He enjoyed himself with cornering a snake. Snakes were very plentiful in the rivers and woods of America, but 95 percent of them were harmless. Young Indians, who have a proclivity to cruelty, select snakes as objects of torture. The reptile is irritated until it bites into a piece of wood and cannot extricate its fangs. Its tormentor seizes the opportunity to impale the snake on the ground by means of a fork consisting of a young tree about four feet long and divested of foliage save one twig near the base. This fork is drawn over the neck of the snake and stuck into the ground. The reptile cannot escape and falls a prey to the myriads of ants which are soon attracted to it! The sting of the ants cause the snake's body to swell to four times its natural dimensions. The snake is gradually choked to death and devoured by the ants which leave nothing behind but a skeleton. As many as half a hundred reptiles are frequently tortured in this manner during the day. The forks are preserved and used for further tortures. Kaan had no eye for the fine garden.

---

the Germans settling in eastern Wisconsin were bold, intellectual, free-thinking "Forty Eighters" – who, like Kiel's founder Henry F. Belitz, fled to the U.S. after the Revolutions (centered in German states but also in other central European countries) failed. Carl Schurz – whose wife started the first Kindergarten in Watertown, Wisconsin - was perhaps the most well-known Forty Eighter, serving as a General in the Civil War, a United States Senator, Lincoln's Minister to Spain and Secretary of the Interior. In another possible nod to Yellowbird, the New York Staatszeitung was also managed by a woman in the 1850s, Anna Uhl.

[47] Published 1855-1880.

Yellowbird and Mrs. Gruen, after sauntering through the garden stepped into the house, where the former felt quite at home. Did Mrs. Gruen know Yellowbird's secrets? They alone could tell. It was certain that Mrs. Gruen thought much of the Indian girl. Mr. and Mrs. Guen had one son who died in Germany at the age of sixteen. His clothes, schoolbooks and other boyish possessions accompanied the parents into the North American wilds. His mother's heart could not be separated from them. Among them was a violin and a lot of notes. Yellowbird, who was totally devoid of prudishness, never waited for any one to beg of her what she was determined to give, and flatly refused what she was resolved not to grant. She immediately seized the violin and played one of the favorite pieces of Edmund, the son of her friend, knowing that there was nothing which could more surely exhilarate Mrs. Gruen who was particularly fond of German folksongs and airs from the Freischuetz. Yellowbird was playing the "Player" from Freischuetz[48]. The soft, sweet, pious tones were reproduced by her in a masterly manner. Mrs. Gruen had never before heard her play in such heavenly fashion. Poor old Mrs. Gruen with the wounded heart, in a strange land, in the depths of the wild virgin forests of America, forever separated from that to her sacred spot, the grave of her son which she had to leave to follow her husband, a fugitive on account of the Revolution of 1848.[49]

Mrs. Gruen was dissolved in tears. When Yellowbird put aside the violin, the old woman, bowed down with grief, staggered over to her and embraced her convulsively.

"Ah, Miss Weber," she sobbed; "why can you not remain with us always?"

"It would but make our parting the sadder," Yellowbird softly replied. "There is no 'Forever' for us mortals." She tenderly embraced Mrs. Gruen and succeeded as usual in consoling her.

---

[48] Freischuetz – Der Freishutz, an opera by Carl Maria von Weber.

[49] Given Goeres' convention for slightly altering real surnames of historical figures for purposes of the story, it is likely Charles Gruening and family who are referenced here. Gruening was amongst those original settlers of New Holstein, Wisconsin who arrived in the U.S.A. with Ferdinand Ostenfeld from Germany in 1848 amidst the turmoil of the Revolutions of 1848, proceeding from New York City to Buffalo to Sheboygan, Wisconsin, to Fond du Lac, Wisconsin and then on to the site of New Holstein via Calumetville. Source: New Holstein Historical Society's webpage "Adventures of the first pioneers"

"No, you are right", Mrs. Gruen said; "there is no 'Forever', but it is cruel when a mother is bereft of her child, her only son, as my Edmund was torn from me." She burst into a flood of tears. Yellowbird again consoled her, saying: "How many a mother is compelled to witness her son wandering into jail or falling a victim to a passion which he combats in vain and which makes him and his kin wretched! In your memory, your Edmund lives on as a good son, noble and dutiful and as such he will follow his dear old mother to the grave, the boundary of joy and grief, where good and bad find equally sweet repose. Suffer your Edmund to repose. He is neither hounded nor driven. He is free from all sorrow, all torment, of which every living being must endure so much. Think of the many sorrows which you have yourself endured! No land will ever make an exile of him. Your Edmund is spared all that. Let him repose, mother Gruen!"

It was evident that Yellowbird's consoling words were not without effect upon Mrs. Gruen who raised up her faithful eyes to the angel on whose breast she had often found solace. Yellowbird again stepped into the open with her aged friend, about whose shoulders she, like a tender daughter, had placed her arm. It was not the third sunny day after the violent rainstorm. Vegetation had begun to sprout and here and there a modest forest flower was peeping out of the last year's withered leaves. The wild pigeons[50] in vast flocks from the south almost darkened the sun. Ducks and geese preferred the night for their flights. During the day they rested at the little lakes, of which there are so many in the beautiful state of Wisconsin, and which, imbedded like gems in the vast forests, were unknown to man, the birds of passage and the wild Indians excepted.

The ponies were grazing peacefully and contentedly when the two good women entered Mrs. Guren's garden. Yellowbird was about to look around for Kaan who, indeed, was in as little danger as a stag of losing his way in the woods, who was to watch lest the ponies raised havoc with Mrs. Gruen's garden, when her sharp eye observed a man leaning against a maple tree. The window of the room, in which Yellowbird had played on the violin, was left open on account of the fine weather. The wanderer had probably been attracted by the captivating tones which the young artiste elicited from the instrument.

---

[50] The once-plentiful and now-extinct passenger pigeon (the last known passenger pigeon died in 1914 at the Cincinnati Zoo).

As soon as the stranger saw Yellowbird's eyes directed toward him, he approached the women, doffed his gray felt hat and begged to be excused for having been caught in the attitude of a listener, saying that he that could resist such tones as he had just heard had no business to dwell among men. The stranger was short and stout and perhaps fifty years of age. His greyish moustache and side-whiskers were cropped close, but his eyes betrayed courage and energy. He was looking for a certain Konrad Weber and had tracked him along the banks of the Wisconsin River to the Dells, where he had lost him. He felt certain of finding him here in the German settlements.

Yellowbird held the old woman's hand firmly in hers. She pressed it lightly, a signal to her to remain silent. The features of the women remained impassive.

"I would have missed the road again," the stranger continued, "if I had not heard the wonderful playing. An Indian lad whom I met in the forest was not to be persuaded to open his lips, and a moment later I hear an Indian girl playing so beautifully on the violin."

"According to your words you are deeply interested in Mr. – Mr. – what did you say his name was?" Yellowbird said naively.

"Konrad Weber, miss," the stranger replied.

"Oh yes, Weber," she said lightly; "I cannot remember having heard of such a party here. But mother Gruen, you know every man, woman and child in this settlement. Do you know a man or a family by that name?" Yellowbird accompanied her words by slightly pressing Mrs. Gruen's hand unobserved by the sharp eye of the detective, for such the stranger was.

"I know a Christoph Weber," said Mrs. Gruen, whose faded hand pressed Yellowbird's as a signal that she understood the peril of the situation. "If you are eager to visit the gentleman, I can describe the way to his abode exactly."

"I am very much obliged to you, madam," he interrupted her; "but first of all I must make certain that your Weber is my Weber. My Weber is a tall man -."

"That my Weber is also," Mrs. Gruen said with a laugh.

"My Weber is about sixty years old," the stranger continued with a smile.

"That my Weber is not," Mrs. Gruen replied; "I am sorry that I must disappoint your hopes. My Weber is a very young man. He is certainly not yet thirty years old."

This report was not a pleasant one to the stranger. He would cheerfully have palmed himself off as a relative of Konrad Weber, in order to gain the confidence of the settlers, but he was not a German. In spite of his trained eye the ladies appeared entirely truthful to him.

"I believe I will have to spend the night in this settlement", he said, and thanking the women for the information received, although it was of no use to him, he saluted and took his leave.

Yellowbird heaved a deep sigh of relief when the stranger disappeared in the forest.

"The traitor does not sleep my uncle always says," Yellowbird muttered; "they are still on our tracks. It seems as though the earth could not keep in her orbit until a portion of her poisoned blood has drunk its fill of the blood of an old man, bowed down with continued persecution. They still hound us."

She could tarry here no longer and called Kaan who was lying on the ground near her cowering like a tiger ready to leap upon his prey. Like a snake Kaan had followed the detective who appeared suspicious to his keen Indian eye. If Shepard had but raised a finger to injure a hair on Yellowbird's head, the Indian would have split his head with the tomahawk which his hand held clutched with a vise-like grip. Even though Mrs. Gruen had not the remotest idea of the intentions of the Indian lad who was now gazing ignorantly over a hawthorn bush, Yellowbird divined his feelings perfectly well. Kaan brought up the ponies, saddled them and Yellowbird mounted Robin with the grace of a professional equestrienne. She congratulated herself upon having brought with her the purchases she had made at the store. After giving Mrs. Gruen some instructions, Yellowbird and Kaan rode away. They did not return the way they had come, but followed a trail which, after a two-mile ride, took them to another trail which crossed the Manitowoc River[51]. After they had entered the forest some distance, Yellowbird halted and asked Kaan: "I believe the spy is on our track; how can we best deceived him?"

Kaan replied: "The stranger is hiding in ambush close to the trail back in the forest. I saw him."

"Let us ride on, my good Kaan; in two hours we will be in camp," Yellowbird said, who had conceived a plan of eluding the sleuth.

---

[51] This would have been a trailing running north of New Holstein and Kiel, likely in the vicinity of Hayton and the Killsnake State Wildlife Area. An Indian trail ran along what is now the route of Highway 151 between Chilton and Manitowoc.

"They are not taking their usual course," the detective muttered to himself; "but do what you please, the old sinner will not escape my clutches this time. The old German fool's five thousand dollars will surely be mine, as well as fees paid by our government. If governments enter into mutual extradition treaties, they must not murmur about the costs. They must be very anxious to get the old fellow back to Germany, for they are hounding him with persistent vigor for eight years now. The flames do not seem to be extinguishing. An American is quicker to forget such a lousy little murder case, especially when there are no dollars in it. Yellowbird did not betray the slightest emotion when I mentioned the name of the murderer. I was anxious to study its effect upon the young comedienne. She is firm as a rock and the young red dog she had with her is descended from an adder. To the devil with our trade which takes us into the wilderness and forces us to frequently fight against apparently invincible obstacles! I will retire after I have performed this task. Nobody can belittle my achievements. I almost regret having addressed the so-called Yellowbird, the Queen of the Indians. And how excellently the old witch played her role! But just wait, it will help them naught. Single-handedly I will send to hell that handful of cowardly red dogs. Yet I am willing to make a bargain with you, Queen of the Chippewas. Give me your little hand and the old thing can creep along unmolested for several years more, until his final repose, among muskrats and other sweet-scented beasts. Your sweet little body is worth the price. Your accomplishments are thrown in with the bargain. Gracious! How that female can handle the fiddle. There's money in that, more than the injured Junkers[52] are willing to pay for the corpse of Doctor Faust[53]. Yellowbird is said to be very much attached to the old sinner. I will try my plan, but not until after I have handcuffed the old man. I'll bet that Yellowbird will accept the bargain. It will rain silver shekels[54] at the gates of the big halls in which the Queen of the Indians will play the violin. I must confess that the scheme charms honey upon my tongue. I was not brought up with delicate attentions and artistic delights; yet what effect did her playing not have upon me! May the devil get me, tooth and nail, if I did not feel like weeping. As far as I can recollect, such a thing did not happen to me before. It is settled, Queen of a copper-hued people, I will trade you for carrion. On the Upper Wisconsin River my luck began. The red beasts were so reticent that their snouts could not have been opened with a crowbar, not even a redhot one. The

---

[52] Prussian aristocrats holding power in what was, in the 19th Century, transforming into modern day Germany.

[53] A reference to Goethe's "Faust" wherein Dr. Faust sells his soul to the devil.

[54] Coins

young adder I met a little while ago was equally silent. Solid, shining gold will loosen many a tongue. With it I loosened the tongue of an announcer of God's word. The fellow was worth being buried alive in alligator mud; yet he furnished me with a clue, which to me is more valuable than the keys of St. Peter."

Such was the soliloquy of Jack Shepard who was hiding behind some bushes close to the trail. He was a detective of the most hardened type. He was at home everywhere and nowhere. His domicile was anywhere where he hung up his hat. He had captured many a desperado. On the Mississippi he had led a wild career. He rather fought than ate. Though unmarried, he was an admirer of the fairer sex. He could drink whiskey as though it was water. To shoot at a man was mere child's play to him. During the past ten years he was a much-feared detective whose services were in good demand.

He arose on account of the heat, he unbuttoned his coat, this revealing a veritable arsenal. In his belt he carried a poniard[55] and half a dozen pistols.

"I will now instruct my men," he murmured to himself, as he walked half a mile towards the village of New Holstein, then turned to the right in the forest and after creeping a few hundred paces through underbrush approached a tent. The latter was made of sail-cloth and could be erected or put away in a few minutes. Near the tent three other fellows of Shepard's caliber were lounging. Shepard, their chief, told them: "It is just as we had suspected from the information given us. The German sinner is among the Chippewas. Today their queen was about. It is a sign that they soon will begin to swarm boys."

"By-Jesus Christ, Jack, it is getting high time that our nerves be given a little excitement. Our sleuth home life is beginning to get tiresome. Let us get the soup-bone after dispatching the beasts guarding it. The vultures and foxes also want to get their living," said one of the company.

"Dave! You talk like a baby," said another of the trio which had awaited their chief in front of the tent; he was a long, bony man with grey hair; emptying his pipe, he said: "If Jack and I talk thus, we would be justified, for we have sent dozens of Indians to their Great Spirit in the Happy Hunting Grounds. We know what they can do; but you have not peopled the heaven of the redskins with a single soul; otherwise you would not talk so damnably contemptuously of them. They say the Indian is a coward. We are pleased to call him so, because he always has to fight against superior numbers and tortures his prisoners. But I tell you, Dave, that the Indian, when pitted man against man, is no coward."

---

[55] A small, slim dagger.

Dave, who was no taller than Shepard and not quite as stout, though no longer young, leaped to his feet and said rather excitedly: "Bill, I give you my word that if I ever get a chance to cast my eye upon such a red dog, he will cease to wander among the living. Do not forget that we did not have a soft snap of it in Mexico."

"Blood and thunder. Close your mouth!" The first of the three spoke, without, however, making a move; "By the living devil, if we were in the midst of a battle, surrounded by giants, you could not carry on worse!" The speaker was an Irishman. He was the shortest of the crowd. His hair was of a fiery red color. His face was beardless and, thanks to small-pox marks, looked like a scraping iron. He too, was over forty years of age. "Chief!" he continued; "say what we had best do. I am tired of this miserable lounging around. It will not be a long time before the mosquitos tackle us."

In the meantime, Shepard had made himself comfortable and lit his pipe. He said after a pause: "Well, the queen arrayed in a very pretty summer garb, flew out today. She was accompanied by a young drone. The bees are never far from the queen. The hive is about seven or eight miles from here.[56] We cannot miss it, as there is but one trail leading to it. I have spoken with the queen. She will report concerning me. I had two objects in view, firstly, to read in her eyes whether our suspicions were well-founded, and, secondly, to induce the Indians to break up camp, in case my first purpose failed. Her eyes remained a sealed book. I might have just as well attempted to gaze through a statue. We must get ready to attack them. What is the best plan now, to pay them a visit in their camp, or to aim at them while they are marching along Indian file? According to our laws, we can shoot down anyone protecting a criminal. Boys, what do I hear of you? Bill, you are the oldest."

---

[56] Given that Gruen's home (and seemingly the detective/bounty hunter campsite) was about two miles west of New Holstein, a location sited seven or eight miles to the east that is also about two miles northeast of Kiel – and is located in an area boggy enough to have tamarack trees – the Native American camp…would seemingly be somewhere in the greater vicinity of the current Kiel Fish and Game location, the broad area around the intersection of Fish and Game Road and Steinthal Road in the Town of Schleswig. One additional note that may be relevant here: there is also an old Native American burial ground on the old Myron Voland farm east of Rockville.

"There is much to be considered," Bill replied. The soup-bone will not of its own accord lie down in our kettle. In a few hours it may be lying in wait for us in its wigwam with a loaded rifle. We may be looking until Christmas to find the wigwam. When the Indians break camp, we can stop them and compel them to deliver up the criminal. But, if he is not with them, we cannot hold them and must let them pass on. The man we are looking for will not be with them. I hope none of you will doubt that".

"Bill, that may be true; but that will not bring us a step further," the chief answered.

"It is not too late," Bill continued; "in two hours our ponies will carry us to the Indian village. Let us surround the nest and watch every move they make. If our bird is to be brought to a place of safety, we have him caged. If they depart with him, we will receive them in military array. We will of course, be disguised as Indians."

"Bill, that is good; he durst not again escape us," the chief said, who immediately uttered a shrill whistle which brought to the spot two young men whom he ordered to bring the horses and then remain quiet until further orders.

"Very likely we shall return in company with our royal highnesses inside of twenty-four hours," the chief said. The two young men were hostlers and had nothing to do with the objects pursued by the sleuths. They had allowed themselves to be persuaded to take part in the expedition, of which they had gotten heartily tired, as they had to look out for provisions for man and beast, cook and look after the dishes and the tent. They had to render implicate obedience. The horses they had to take care of were like the Indian's ponies, but better fed and stronger.

In ten minutes the bold knights were on their way to the hostile Indian village, where on the morning of that day such sweet and peaceful songs had been sent to heaven by the children. The four fellows pretended to be fur-traders, as it was the season of the year in which the Indians sold their surplus furs and hides, and none of the settlers considered it anything out of the ordinary to give them information about the way to the Indian camp, their numbers, etc. No one, however, could give them any information about an old white man.

Yellowbird and Kaan had reached their camp in less then two hours. While Kaan was unloading the horse, Yellowbird rode directly to Solomon and counseled with him. She then stopped before Caqua's wigwam. The latter emerged out of it unbidden like a lion out of this den. Yellowbird extended her hand which the savage caressed and spoke to him. What she said, must have been something extraordinary, for his frightful face beamed with joy and death and destruction blazed from his eyes, Yellowbird rode to her wigwam as unconcerned as though nothing unpleasant had happened. She was certain that the stranger had accomplices, but their number was unknown to her.

XVI. THE FUGITIVE.

In the vicinity of Sheboygan Falls, which is a suburb of Sheboygan and is situated on the Sheboygan River where the latter has a considerable falls, there stood a log cabin. Its environment betrayed signs of cultivation. The land had been partially cleared. The interior of the cabin was marked by extraordinary neatness and orderliness. The lower story comprised a kitchen, parlor and two sleeping rooms. Of the latter there were six in the upper story. It was to be seen at a glance that feminine hands had here created a cozy home. In the parlor two old men sat at a common table. They had just finished a game of cards. Schlicht[57], the owner of the house, was the winner. While putting the cards away, he said: "Now, Fichte[58], we are square again," and turning to the kitchen, "Elisa, if you please, Fichte and I have concluded an armistice until tomorrow noon."

Mrs. Schlicht, a woman of fifty-eight years[59], who was well-preserved and still showed traces of former extraordinary beauty, stepped out of the kitchen and brought in coffee and biscuit on a tray. The two old men would not permit her to go to the trouble of spreading a table-cloth. Mrs. Schlicht passed around the coffee cups and the trio emptied them while conversing freely.

Since the death of his wife, year in and year out, Fichte appeared regularly every afternoon at the home of his dear friend and neighbor and played pique[60] with him. Although stakes were never put up, they enjoyed the game as much as ever.

---

[57] This is Johann Reinhard Schlichting, who settled in the Town of Sheboygan Falls in 1843. He was the father of Mrs. Helen Belitz, Reinhard Schlichting, Herman Schlichting and Johanna Schlichting - and father-in-law of Henry F. Belitz.

[58] This is Friedrich Ficthen, father of Yellowbird's love interest, Friedrich "Fritz" Fichten.

[59] This is Elise W. Schlichting, wife of Johann Reinhard Schlichting. She was born in Oldenburg, Lower Saxony (Germany) in 1806. Her stated age of 58 doesn't quite align with the story taking place in 1859, as she would have been 53 at the time. She moved to Kiel in 1847 with her son, Reinhard Schlichting and lived there until 1866 before moving to Chilton.

[60] Also "Piquet" - a two-player trick-taking card game that originated in France. Here it is seemingly a symbol that the two players are learned and of high class, as the game was typically played by aristocrats and the upper class. The popular traditional German/Wisconsin card game of Sheepshead uses the 32-card "Piquet deck".

"Did I understand you correctly, Reinhardt? Has Konrad Weber turned up again?" Mrs. Schlicht asked.

"No, dear wife; he has not turned up; but now and then we read about him in the New York Staatszeitung," Schlicht answered.

"The report says nothing further than the old Von Ferdung, in spite of his bodily infirmity, perseveres in having Konrad Weber persecuted with the same fury as in former years, regardless of cost. His heart will not stop beating until Weber is captured and surrendered—dead or alive—to justice. In this country little attention is paid to the political red tape, which in Germany is close on the verge of fetish-worship, nor to the death of isolated individuals, the victims of political friction. That in Philadelphia Dr. Weber had to kill three men in order to defend himself, must be ascribed to the persistent persecution to which he was subjected even on this side of the Atlantic. You say, my dear Fichte, that our land, that is, our government, does not pay much attention to such things. Weber was persecuted as a murderer by Germany. There was no question about politics. Germany and the United States extradite heavy offenders. In Philadelphia, where Weber was living under an assumed name peacefully and contentedly with his attractive little niece, he was attacked in a moment when he was giving little Meta instructions in music. Volkwart, a Berlin detective, brought with him to this country the one-eyed Pottgiesser, who had been in this country before, travelled through California, where he lost an eye, and lived in Hamburg. These two searched for Weber and at last called in as an aid the Irish policeman Mike Quinn, after they had made sure that their man was living in Philadelphia. In his own house Weber shot Volkward and dashed out the Irishman's brains with a chandelier, when the latter tried to arrest him."

"That was the way it was, Schlicht," Fichte interrupted; "but it never came to a trial in this country. If it would have come to a trial, Weber could have shown that Walter von Ferdung, son of Gustave Adolph von Ferdung, was slain by him as a result of a political altercation, when the waves of the suppressed Revolution of 1848 were still surging high. In that case Weber would not have been delivered up by the government of the United States."

Schlicht replied: "Fichte, you are mistaken and very seriously. The warrant charged murder, committed by Konrad Weber upon Walter von Ferdung in a restaurant at Oldenburg and all the papers captured Weber, he would have been compelled to travel back with them without mercy to Germany. Political criminals are not delivered up, but murderers do not come under that category."

"I do not call Weber's action murder," said Schlicht.

"I cannot understand," Mrs. Schlicht now said, "how two such educated men as Lieutenant von Ferdung and Dr. Konrad Weber can have became so excited in a coffee house about political questions that they had resort to murderous weapons."

Fichte, a very thin man with white hair, arose and told the story of the affair with such pathos that the fire which drove him from his old home became very comprehensible: "Neighbors! Just think of a man like Dr. Weber, a man who spent his life doing useful things, a man who told the servants of a Count von Schalten who were sent to bring him to his lordship's bedside in a carriage 'Gottlieb Kermer is in dire need, but your gracious lord is not. After Kermer has been attended to, I will come to the Count afoot.' He was a man who could attend to a day laborer in preference to a king; a man whom his oppressed fellows almost deified. Such a man should calmly pocket from a scamp like Lieutenant von Ferdung words like these: 'If you do not close your fodder-trap, you will get boxed on the ears.'"[61]

This theme was frequently discussed in the Schlicts' house, where otherwise perpetual harmony reigned. It never failed to strain every nerve of Fichte's worn-out body. The haggard old man raised himself to his full height. Once more the fire of youth seemed to animate him and as loudly as he could he rehearsed the scene between the lieutenant and the doctor in the restaurant. Fichte continued his recital as follows: "'Come here, you fellow', said the doctor; 'you unfledged booby! If you were none, you would respect a man of my age, who became what he is through restless striving. You like others of your ilk fancy that nobler blood courses through your veins. Insanity seems to be hereditary. The Jews, who are otherwise very prudent people, buy an inkspot out of your fool's pond and carry on likewise. It seems to delight them. But if this noble blood is subjected to an exact analysis, one will find it equal to that of a Gypsy that is, if the noble drop it as fresh and healthy as a Gypsy's. If, then, such a young fellow has nothing else to show that such noble blood flows in his veins, for which he has nothing to show but a meaningless birth certificate — a ridiculous amount of monkey certificate would express it more truly — which is even an object of barter, such a young man is a booby and does not belong to the society of men of action. If you still entertain any desire to box ears, do not do violence to your feelings. You know, I am a physician and know many remedies, among others an excellent one for young fools.' So saying, Weber made a strong pantomime motion with his right hand, symbolic of a forceful slap."

[61] It is not entirely clear what precise text is intended in this section; clearly, Weber is seen here by Fichte as a radical egalitarian/anti-aristocrat who embodied certain principles of the failed Revolutions of 1848. It is unclear what, if any, of the stories presented in this chapter are true or based on true events.

"The lieutenant's face turned purple. He seemed to have fallen into catalepsy while Doctor Weber was thus lecturing to him from another table. All of a sudden life appeared to return into the inert mass. The lieutenant drew his sword and rushed toward the physician, who sat calmly on his chair and exclaimed: "You revolutionary coward and quack for dog rabble!"

"When Weber beheld the enraged fellow rushing toward him, he grasped his half-emptied wine bottle, dodged the lieutenant's wild blow and hit him on the uncovered head with all his might. The lieutenant expired after remaining in a condition of unconsciousness for four days. And for this deed I will bless him with my dying breath."

The recital had exhausted Fichte. He was no longer young and fate had played him many a prank. Excitement wore him out and his days were almost numbered.

"It is too bad that the young man did not regain consciousness. Perhaps he might have gotten his Gustav Adolph into a more pleasurable mood with the confession that he himself provoked the quarrel, especially as an investigation later on showed that Dr. Weber and Professor Ulerich had carried on a harmless conversation on scientific topics," Mrs. Schlicht said.

"Dear Elisa," Schlicht replied; "it was even proved that the fellow was itching for an opportunity to start a quarrel with the doctor. The cause of the animosity was said to have been due to the fact that the doctor bestowed upon the lieutenant's father even less of his scant courtesy than he did upon Count von Schalten. He handed the body-servant of the lieutenant's father a note inscribed with the words: 'Eat and drink less and work more! I do not treat loafers. Dr. Weber.'"

"My God! What language from a scholar!" Mrs. Schlicht exclaimed.

"But these expressions contain truth, Mrs. Schlicht," Fichte said; "the entire lazy brood of vermin, which can do nothing but eat and drink should be exterminated. About a fortnight thereafter another physician, a professor on the University of Bonn, was called in. It was said that he could cure anything and had swallowed wisdom by the bushel basket. Yet whenever a really critical operation had to be performed, the hated Dr. Weber was invariably called in. Professor Ulerich paid no attention to the rabble and got by on the grace of God and by maintaining very friendly relations with his colleague, Dr. Weber, whose great abilities and learning he publicly acknowledged, to the disgust of the overbearing drones."

Fichte had worked himself into a very tender mood and closed his effusion with an allusion to the doctor's noble actions, accentuating the fact that he frequently sent his bill to rich people with the remark to remit the account to the poor-fund. His object was to invite the rich to assist the needy.

The small assembly of good old people were in a mild frame of mind. They knew the good doctor personally and loved and respected him.

"Yes," Mr. Schlicht added, "it is so. Such a great, noble, and able man is hounded by sleuths as though he were a cannibal. All on account of a whim arising in the mind of a bloated good-for-nothing."

Mrs. Schlicht then said: "I wonder where the poor doctor is now staying. As long as he lives, he will probably remain a hounded fugitive, for the large sums promised by Gustav Adolph to his captors will make the sleuths even in this free country anxious for the blood money. I am convinced that the doctor will never re-cross the ocean alive. His fate is to be deplored for two reasons, for it is linked to that of his very pretty little niece. Whenever they speak of Dr. Weber, I must think of the handsome and intelligent pretty little Meta. What pains did not the doctor take to educate the girl! When barely nine years old she was even then very proficient on the piano and violin. The little southern girl delighted me."

"That is true, my dear wife," Schlicht added; "but you must also consider that her uncle, the doctor, was an instructor the like of whom can not easily be found. My God! How rapturously the man could play the violin! Do you remember, Fichte, how in 1847, in the famine year, he arranged a charity concert in Oldenburg, at which he contributed his share for the benefit of the sufferers?"

"Certainly I remember," Fichte replied; "it is strange that in some persons many talents will develop so splendidly while in others there will be an absolute dearth of them. Nature at times distributes her gifts in a very step-motherly fashion. Talent seems to be hereditary in the Weber family. What did not Bernhard Weber, Konrad's father, accomplish in the line of mechanics? How many extraordinary improvements did not owe their origin to his skillful hand? What an excellent mariner was not Gerhardt Weber, Meta's father," Schlicht added, "if he had remained alive at least his poor, helpless child would not be effected by the persecution of Weber. She will not leave her uncle."

"O God! The poor thing!" Mrs. Schlicht said in a tone that betrayed that her motherly heart was deeply moved and added that Meta's mother died shortly before her father. "I would like to have seen the woman. She is said to have been of rare beauty and either a Portuguese or a Creole."[62]

---

[62] Yellowbird/Meta Weber's description as a "southern" European girl and this reference to her partial Portuguese or mixed "Creole" background may be an attempt to indicate that her complexion was slightly darker than the average German immigrant to Wisconsin and explain why her appearance amidst Native Americans may have seemed less remarkable to a casual observer than if she had been of purely Germanic background.

Schlicht replied that she was very likely a Creole. He had seen women of that type, among whom there were some of ravishing beauty, and that Meta's eyes and hair gave evidence of Creole descent.

"We are always speaking of a child," Mrs. Schlicht remarked; "but do you know that she is now fully nineteen years old, or about three years older than our Johanna."

"I guess that's right, Elisa," Schlicht confirmed the calculations of his wife; "whether the woman was Portuguese or Creole or even a quadroon[63], the fact remains that her death broke Gerhardt Weber's heart. Without his Pedrea[64] his life was devoid of purpose. His wealth offered him no consolation and he soon followed her into the realms beyond."

Fichte, who appeared very feeble and seemed to be dreaming, hastily put the question: "Will the innocent girl be robbed of her property in Germany as we were robbed of ours?"

Schlicht was able to give some information on the subject, for he had ascertained that Meta's fortune was guarded by Professor Ulerich, who, he said, was well-posted on the affairs of Dr. Weber and his niece and, since he could do nothing further for his colleague, took the more interest in the girl. He administered her estate according to law and the wishes of Dr. Weber himself, who was Meta's guardian.

"How old was little Meta when her father brought her to his brother to take care of her?" Mrs. Schlicht asked her husband.

"A trifle over four years," he replied.

"We thought that the doctor would leave the care of the little one entirely to his housekeeper, because he had never been married and did not care to busy himself with children, but oh, how we were deceived! How the man clung to the child! Perhaps he is doing better than we imagine. The old von Ferdung is said to have become crazed by the death of his son. Reinhardt! Consider he was his only son; think of our own children who rest beneath the sod," Mrs. Schlicht said.

Here again the mother was speaking and the voice of politics and even science must then remain silent.

---

[63] A person of one quarter mixed black or African heritage.

[64] Literally, "fight with stones" – likely a Spanish or Portuguese name for Yellowbird/Meta's mother.

Schlicht, the thick, short, good-hearted man, seized his wife's hand, saying: "It is true, Elisa; let them all rest. The sleepers are to be envied. Our good friend Dr. Weber will undoubtedly be able to get along very well in spite of the persecution. While fleeing from this old man, he palmed himself off as the husband of a shoemaker's wife who was following her husband. In the railway depot he discarded his own suit for a faded one belonging to the shoemaker, for which the woman had no room in her trunk and which she therefore carried in a bundle. Thus disguised the doctor was able to deceive the inspectors and land safely at New York as Shoemaker Metzer, father of ten children, exclusive of his Meta. I am convinced that the shoemaker's wife had no reason to regret the event. He showed the passports whenever they were demanded and generally held one or even two of the Metzer hopefuls on his knees."

Schlicht now came to speak of the recent events in Kiel. Young Kleinschmidt had came on horseback to Sheboygan Falls and brought the news that their son Herman was improving in health; also of the break into the dam, where Friedrich Fichte had distinguished himself in a heroic manner. Schlicht took his old friend by the hand and said: "Your Friedrich has been a source of great joy to you, Fichte. His energy and practical sense promise a bright future for him in this country."

The messenger reported that besides the settlers even Indians assisted in saving the dam. A chief's daughter by the name of Yellowbird had heard the first alarm and come upon the scene with the entire band of Indians roaming about Kiel. The Indians are said to have toiled like beavers.

Fichte thought that somebody must have put a flea into the boy's ear, as Indians never worked.

"I am glad, however," Schlicht said, "that all went well, for I know what efforts it cost Behl to build the dam. In about fourteen days the plankroad is expected to be in a passable condition. The bridge is also to be completed at that time. Our children will visit us then. A team can now get through from here to Howard's Grove. We will have to wait until then for detailed news. Our Johanna will teach school. The school year will embrace two more months this season. Although our experiences in the old country were terrible, yet the pleasure we take in our children is equally great, here or elsewhere, and that is about all that keeps up old age. It is a pleasure permeating equally deep into the breast of the parents, whether they reside in a palace in some great capital or a log cabin in the forest depths of strange lands."

"I am glad that they are all doing well," said Fichte; "Johanna is a neat and good child and will as a teacher do more than her duty. I would like to live until the day when I could hail her as a daughter-in-law, but here" — pointing to his breast — "it is going downhill with giant steps." So saying, he pointed out at an opening, and continued: "The hummock under yonder tamarack, where my dear Dora rests, draws me all too powerfully to it." The old man wept, and Schlicht and his wife were also deeply moved. Fichte continued: "Thither you will soon convey me, without song and noise, to my dear Dora. During life we clung firmly and faithfully together. We belong together also in far America, under the tamarack."

The Feeble old man who occupied a log cabin at the edge of the clearing and after whose wants his dear old friend Friedrich looked, staggered back to his lonely abode, after pressing the hands of his friends. Schlicht silently grasped his wife's hand and stepped with her to the window, from which Mrs. Fichte's grave could be seen. Fichte walked totteringly to his cabin, took a glance at the hummock containing the remains of her who was dearest to him in life, and entered his dwelling, muttering to himself: "I will soon be with you, Dora."

To his wife, Schlicht said: "Who would believe that in the breast of that faded old man there once glowed such fiery passion for his fellow beings and his country!"

Fichte's words proved true. Six weeks later his neighbors carried him from his lone log cabin to that tamarack, beneath whose shade he now rests in peace and quiet with his spouse.

XVII. THE DUEL.

Deep quiet reigned in and about the Indian village. Nature, too, was at rest. Not a leaf was stirring. The needles of the pines had ceased their whispering. The moonless sky displayed a few isolated stars whose faint and distant light was unable to penetrate the dense foliage of the forest. The gurgling of the brook, which flowed past near the village and had been swollen by the recent rains, was the only sound that interrupted the nightly stillness.

Toward evening, a pock-marked fur-trader had visited the village. He was bound to see the queen and inspect the mysterious wigwam, but the queen was "not at home" and the wigwam remained closed to him. Pona and Kaan stood guard at the two wigwams and attended to their business earnestly and courageously. The wigwams were as sacred to them as their palaces are to millionaires.

"Our pelts and furs are already sold to Milwaukee," Kaan said fearlessly; "the traders are cheaters: they do not get our furs."

"Pup, guard your snout; otherwise I shall take your hide with me and cut it up into strings," the trader replied.

The frivolity of the rough customer's remarks was unable to intimidate the boys. They were as unsusceptible to his arguments as were the surrounding groves. The pretended fur-trader was courageous as well as crafty. The unconcerned attitude of the boys, who spoke a surprisingly good English, led him to suppose that gun barrels were aimed at him from ambush and that he was liable to become personally acquainted with their contents as soon as he handled any of the lads roughly. He had no desire, however, for a perforated body and there was no course left open to him except to retreat.

Some twenty minutes later the sleuth and his companions were gathered at an appointed spot. Exchanging their discoveries, they had to confess that thus far they had made no headway. The only hope they still cherished was that Konrad Weber was still sojourning in the camp of the redskins, for they had not found another trail leading out of the camp.

The sleuths regaled themselves with victuals which they carried with them in oblong packages fastened to the backs of the saddles. They also partook liberally of whiskey. They decided to attack the two wigwams at night. In order to rest their bodies for the task before them, they stretched themselves out on the grass in the forest. Their plan was thus: Shepard was to force his way unseen into the two wigwams and the three others were to shoot down anyone crossing their path. Shepard threatened anyone who should touch a hair of Yellowbird's with dire vengeance. They all knew the ground. They were to be about one hundred feet apart when they proceeded to the attack of the wigwams, but the assault was to be undertaken jointly. In case of there actually being eight or ten Indian warriors in the nest, it would not mean much, for each one of the assailants was able to fire any number of shots, each of which was sure to level a redskin.

Shepard's calculation was as follows: "From the east and west I am secure from hostile bullets since I will be between the two wigwams. My helpers will be to the north of me. Consequently I will be in danger only from the south and darkness will shield me there. If the Indians really expected an attack (of which he, by the way, entertained no doubt), they would shoot from behind the shelter of trees in the distance. Let them shoot! Trees and bushes are so thick about the wigwams that the Indian's bullets will not hit me. Before the Indians have had a chance to reload, I will be with the old man in a safe place."

All seemed favorable to Shepard. Bell, the tall Yankee, would have preferred to do the job by daylight. Of course, they had the advantage that the Indians could not take a sure aim by night and had to shoot in the direction from which they heard a noise, also, that the Indians find more difficulty by night in loading their guns.

In New Holstein the fur-traders had procured two gallons of whiskey which they carried with them in a rubber pouch which formed the center of attraction for them. They partook freely of the liquor. The sun was setting. In three hours they were to begin with their enterprise. At daylight, Shepard expected to reach his tent with his sweet and rich booty. He was reclining against a tree and puffing huge volumes of smoke out of his pipe. The horses were standing in a dense cluster of trees. They were accustomed to go without fodder for a day or two and yet run with their usual speed.

Shepard gave himself up to his thoughts. He thought differently from the way in which he had spoken. He knew that he had committed a great mistake. The violin and the eyes were the cause of it. He could escape from heavenly tones after he had heard them; but from those eyes — never! They had fascinated him. Shepard stood motionless while his mind wandered. He wanted to see the fair creature tremble when he mentioned the name of Konrad Weber, he wanted to see Yellowbird on her knees before him, and then draw her up to him, embrace her in his arms and whisper to her that her uncle might live, that Yellowbird should live and be happy, if she would consent to become his wife.

Experienced and well-informed as Shepard was, he had failed to take into consideration Yellowbird's youthful heart. He knew very well that he ought to have entered the Indian camp while his purposes were still unknown. At that time Yellowbird's uncle had no security except his hiding place, but now preparations for his defense had been made, Shepard also knew very well that if he had undertaken the attack in the afternoon, neither he nor one of his comrades would now be among the living. At the same time, he had to confess to himself, the enterprise would have been a trivial matter to execute a day sooner. How easily could not his Irishman or he himself disguised as a fur trader, have convinced himself of the time when the Indians went hunting. Without trouble they could have captured their man and walked off with him.

"I am one day behind - one full day," Shepard muttered to himself; "Yesterday I had not yet heard Yellowbird's violin play, I had not yet beheld her eyes — those divine lights. How differently these would have gazed at me, if I had been able to offer their owner a big price for them!"

Shepard took deep draughts out of the liquor flask and continued his meditations: "Who can blame Konrad Weber for defending himself, especially as he knows that money is all we are after? What do we care whether a lousy JUNKER[65] cools his vengeance or not? Why doesn't the old dotard do his own fighting, as the doctor has done? Instead, they throw away money by the handful and buy sleuths. They say the officers merely perform their duty. O the devil! Duty! If the German lord had been a beggar or day laborer, they could have strangled his wife and children and no cock would have crowed about it. Doctor! Defend yourself bravely, if you have no desire to go to Germany. I cannot blame you for wishing to remain here. We are accursed sleuths! Each of us has more to account for than you. They say you are a right good fellow and committed no crime except to defend yourself when you are attacked. You think more of yourself than others do, and have remained true to yourself to this very day. I remember very well the history of your case as reported in the newspapers. They made you out a noble fellow who, by virtue of extradition treaties between Germany and the United States, must be delivered up. It is a shame that two men should for money's sake be delivered up to bloated purses. Yet, he that has said A must also say B. My purpose must be accomplished, for a higher prize than the plutocrat's gold is beckoning. The violin and Yellowbird's beautiful eyes!"

The bulky sausage-shaped rubber flask containing the whiskey grew thinner and thinner as the night advanced. The sleuths were evidently equally matched as far as ability to consume the fiery beverage was concerned. Their faces became bloated. When filled up with liquor they were veritable bloodhounds. Their victim is lost when they have his scent. Such, too is generally the fate of him whom such sleuths are tracking. When they have once smelled blood, its shedding becomes their main object, especially when worked up by the demon of drink.

The fellows were not inconvenienced by the darkness. They found their favorite beverage as well without sunshine. Nothing was stirring. While the sleuths were resting, not even a dog barked.

Scarcely twenty paces away from the camp of the sleuths lay a coil that seemed lifeless. Two big hands lying flat on the ground on either side of the colossus gave it the appearance of a giant turtle. On top, where one had reason to suppose the location of a head, two spots were visible. They were small in comparison to the monster, but emitted weird sparks of fire.

---

[65] Prussian (German) aristocrat. Here, Shepard's employer.

The fiercest lion or grizzly bear would have started back like a timid lamb at the sight of this monster; a reptile of the most dangerous kind would have fled precipitously. Yet on the breast of the monster lay a surpassingly handsome girl, like a tender, sleeping angel, and whispered into its ear with a sweet voice what the sleuths were intending to do. She had listened to their counsels and heard all. She had no fear of the monster's claws. For a time she had placed one of her soft hands into them and the monster seemed to be pleased. Silently as she had come she left the monster to itself. An hour had passed. With the exception of the activity of its fiery orbs, the monster seemed an inert mass, so still it lay.

"Bill, it is now eleven o'clock, the nest must be raided," Shepard whispered to his neighbor; "Don't forget that we keep track of each other by the gentle breaking of a twig. Shoot down all that cross your path."

"If every member of the redskinned brood does not resemble a coal-sieve by tomorrow, I will be roasted. Tomorrow the vultures will fly to their lairs with the entrails of the red dogs," Bill replied.

Bill had been quite a promising youth with a fair education, but had fallen into bad company and turned out a robber and an assassin.

The Irishman had taken off his coat and put it softly away. After taking a deep drink at the whiskey flask he cautiously crept into the thicket. Dan followed the Irishman's example in every particular and was getting into the position marked out for him. None of the sleuths had any fear. Shepard told them while they were proceeding to assault the village: "The night seems to be an ideal one for our butterfly hunt. Do not touch the girl under any circumstances." To himself he muttered: "I would rather place her on another throne."

"Good bye, boss," Bill said, after shoving a tremendous quid of tobacco into his mouth.

"Good bye, Bill, take care," Shepard replied.

"Well, Shepard, I guess we have gone through different trials before Uncle Sam conferred knighthood upon us," Bill retorted.

Shepard's course was the shortest route to the wigwams. He had, therefore, ample time to take another drink. The quantities of liquor those fellows could consume was a marvel.

Shepard now also relieved himself of his coat and his arms glittered in the darkness. He knew his way without looking. He was an expert in all he undertook. His nerves and courage were like steel.

As soon as Jack Shepard set himself in motion, life seemed to return into the body of the monster, whose claws began to raise themselves. Immediately the monster resumed his cowering position. With head bent forward and claws extended from the side of the body, the monster moved forward quite as rapidly as the detective, but in spite of his bulk as silently as a worm.

Bill had just broken a twig and Shepard answered the signal. At the same moment Shepard fancied himself transplanted into the mountain forests of Guinea, for before him stood, stiff as a statue, a gigantic gorilla. He stepped back a pace and put his iron hand on the butt of a pistol. The gorilla made a stride forward and both were in the same relative position again.

Shepard's blood seemed to freeze in his veins. Such a monster he had never seen. Yet his natural courage, aided by the liquor he had drunk, asserted its supremacy and he reached for a pistol. At the same moment one claw of the monster clutched his throat and the other his right hand. In the darkness of a Wisconsin forest a wrestling more terrible than can be pictured, ensued. The wild gorilla clutched tightly what he had once grasped. Until now no one had ever vanquished him and he had been in many desperate encounters. Jack Shepard had an advantage over his antagonist, because he could still freely move his left arm. He was about to reach for his knife. In his claws the monster felt the pulsation of every nerve of his foe. With the agility of a tiger he had pressed Shepard against a tree so that he could not extend his arm for the knife.

Shepard's eyes were bursting from their sockets. His breast appeared to be on the verge of outbursting. With his left hand he aimed blows at the body of his foe who dodged them successfully. He then placed his foot against the tree, and, exerting his utmost strength from top to toe, managed to give his body a swing. Both combatants touched the ground. Shepard was the under body. The giant now sought to break Shepard's right hand and then to repeat the experiment with the left; but, although he was endowed with the strength of a hellhound, it was not an easy task, for Shepard's body was like steel.

Shepard was convinced that it was the giant's purpose to kill him as he had himself killed many a victim, by strangling him without giving him an opportunity to utter a sound in order to avoid a rain of bullets from the rear. The giant's touch therefore, at Shepard's neck tightened; his thumb had already sunk deep into Shepard's neck. The Strangling contest of the two Herculeses in the dense thicket made no more commotion that the cooing of two lovers. It lasted but a minute.

Although Shepard's face had already turned blue, the crisis had not yet come. Shepard once more strained to the utmost all of his huge muscular strength and succeeded in getting on his feet. Curiously, he found himself in the same position as before, leaning against the tree. Shepard now tried to get a firm hold to tear out the monster's entrails, but he succeeded as little in that as in reaching one of his many weapons. In spite of the colossus hanging to his body, Shepard again bobbed up with the result that the gorilla was under him. Yet before Shepard could draw a gun, both were on their feet again. A moment later they were again tugging away at each other on the ground.

Both contestants were exerting to the last degree of tension every nerve and every muscle. Their motions were comparable to the inexplicable jerking movements of decapitated poultry, probably the result of great muscular exertion.

The two dark figures continued to wrestle and came near a half-decayed log close to the brook. Into it both of the fighters, who had not uttered a sound during the struggle, fell. The horrible battle was there decided.

After a brief while Caqua[66], the victor, crawled up the bank of the brook, drew his hunting-knife from his belt and scraped the mud off his leggings. The water in the brook had been colored black as ink during the strangling battle by the upheaval of the mud at its bottom, and was beginning to get clearer.

Caqua gazed down at his victim. His face, which resembled a big skull, showed a satisfied grin whenever Shepard's corpse appeared on the surface of the water. Shepard's neck, into which Caqua's claws had sunk deep, displayed all colors and was greatly swollen. His right wrist was but a lump of raw meat. The hand itself was crushed.

Caqua considered this deed as the first one worth mentioning which he had performed for his guardian angel. It caused him nameless joy. He vividly conjured up in his mind the scene where Yellowbird — then a mere child — saved him from death by slow torture while he was tied hands and feet and standing "in the pillory".

Today he at length had found an opportunity to return the favor. He had preformed his task well. The corpse at the bottom of the creek bore evidence to it. If he only could slay a man per day for her, the queen of his tribe! He could see no wrong in that. Remorse was foreign to his animal nature, especially for a deed done upon her request. He would most cheerfully have despoiled the corpse or at least seized Shepard's weapons — but she had prohibited it. Taking a last look at Shepard's remains, Caqua, happier than a victorious hero, sauntered slowly toward his wigwam.

---

[66] And now we know the identity of the "gorilla" monster.

XVIII. THE DEBATE.

"Do not touch any of your weapons! Rifles are aimed at you. I will not be unjust to you. Let us have fair play. You see that I am unarmed," said a very tall man to Bill, who was standing directly in front of him. The calmness and the firm voice of the speaker had quite an effect on the ruffian who was somewhat nonplussed. However, his innate rowdyism and impudence, stirred up by the huge quantity of liquor he had imbibed, soon asserted their supremacy, and he replied: "I am a federal officer and never enter into a compromise. Neither do I allow anyone to cross my path. I am accustomed to travel them unhindered. In order that we may correctly understand each other, let me inform you that the officers of such a firm acknowledge no obstacle."

"You are here on neutral ground," the stranger answered; "for these lands have not yet been placed to us by others. The government has not yet decided this question. I ask you now, what business have you in our village at midnight. If your calling brings you here. Please show your credentials."

Bill responded: "The papers throwing light upon our actions are in the possession of my chief. The credentials you ask for may be a great surprise to you, because, judging from your fine language, I suspect that you are the bird we are looking for. Your head is very much in demand."

"If Konrad Weber is the man you refer to," the stranger replied, "your suppositions are correct. I, too, have a desire, and that is to retain my head. In this respect I have not yet been able to change my taste to suit that of others."

"But on my side is our great country," Bill threw in, who began to understand whom he was confronting.

Weber continued: "On my side there is only one man, but who has the same rights as your country. Your country and I owe our existence to the very same creation. This creation, however, gave to none of its creatures more rights than to another. Your firm is to afford none of its creatures more rights than to another. Your firm is anxious to kill me. My firm, on the contrary, desires to live. You see, we are again confronted by the same question. You are risking no more than what is demanded of me — life, the right to continue to exist as a human being."

"But, sir, criminals must be judged," Bill groaned, while attempting to clutch one of his weapons. Weber calmly placed his hand on the sleuth's arm, giving the latter a sample of his prowess which appeared suspicious to Bill who was waiting for succor from his accomplices. Where were they? According to the prearranged plan, they ought to have been at hand by this time, as he had but a few moments ago heard the breaking of a twig, the concerted signal. If Bill had been able to see who gave the signal, his hair would have stood on end. It was Kaan who gave the signal. Yellowbird had posted him as to how and when to do so. She could place implicit reliance on her followers.

"Sir, who has told you that I am a criminal?" Dr. Weber asked the sleuth after the latter had again assumed a respectful position.

"The warrant charges you with the killing of several people, of whom one was a citizen of this country," Bill blubbered out.

"Napoleon Bonaparte and Frederich the Great killed many more persons than I have killed, yet both were very much respected," Weber said.

"But no warrants were issued against them," answered Bill who was growing more uneasy every moment.

"That is, indeed, true. They stood above the law. If all of those who were conducted to the slaughter pen by those two men had had the power to determine their own actions, they would undoubtedly have remained alive for at least some time longer. It was sheer force that drove those poor fellows into death. At this very moment I am confronted by a power which seeks to drive me into death. Do you not find it very natural that I offer opposition?"

"You are not opposing my personal power," said Bill, "but those who have imposed my duties upon me."

Weber replied: "The extent of your duty and how much thereof you are disposed to carry out is a matter for you alone to determine. Right must yield to force. Every man must be pleased with those rights which a power prescribes for him. I am now prepared to put force against force or right against right, as you please. Lay down your arms and my projected game may commence." He spoke without betraying the slightest sign of excitement.

Bill answered: "My chief, Mr. Shepard, must be here with his men at any moment. You may parley with him."

"Your chief, provided he is still among the living, will be altogether too busy at present to put in an appearance. His men are in a like predicament. Our queen has made all necessary arrangements to have each one of you taken in charge by a decent reception committee. It fell to my lot to accord you a formal reception. Our queen is just. She pitted man against man. But, if the vultures are to feed by daybreak their young with our entrails, as you asserted a short while ago, it is time that we came to that point. The others may have won or lost their game by this time. At any rate, let us not be laggards. In case you should loose, it would be too bad about the snug sum which is set upon my head. But, since a game is a game, we must take our chances. I have nothing but my life to put up."

While Weber was pronouncing this argument, cold chills overran Bill. He saw death staring him in the face. He knew that his colleagues were corpses, and that they had very likely died without the aid of metaphysical dissertations. He felt that Dr. Weber recognized in him a man who had received a good education and was desirous of preparing him for the worst, from the standpoint of natural right. He knew that they were betrayed. In his soul he cursed the stupidity of his chief. He waited no longer for his fellows. He knew that each one had to fight for his life.

"You ought to know, Dr. Weber, that you have to obey the laws. Every decent person does so. I therefore demand of you to follow. In the name of the United States of America, I arrest you," Bill said.

"Now, I say, in the name of the United States of America, you are arrested. So, you see, we are squared again," Dr. Weber repeated mockingly.

"If you are a decent man, you will obey my command," Bill retorted.

Weber answered: "Since there is no way in which we can come to an agreement and since our words of honor will probably not be called into requisition, there is nothing left for us but a battle, or a game, as I am pleased to call it. We may look upon our affair as we please. We always run up against the same problem — the question of division. Power drove me out of my native land. Power robs of land and wealth. Power dethrones even monarchs. Power decides every struggle. Since you will not let me wander my paths in peace, I will declare war against you. Until I have counted three, I will attack you on neutral ground."

Dr. Weber had barely finished, when a pistol gleamed in the sleuth's hand. The latter, however, did not size up his adversary correctly, for before he could discharge his weapon, the doctor smashed his jaw with a blow of his ponderous fist. Bill tottered, blood streamed from his eyes and noise. He raised his weapon again and a bullet lightly grazed the doctor's shoulder.

"Miserable coward!" Weber exclaimed; "is this the manner in which you intend to feed your vultures?"

The doctor's eyes were flaming with rage. With a second blow he felled the sleuth who made a desperate effort to get on his feet and raise his pistol. The doctor caught him by the throat, wrestled the pistol from his hand and said: "Dog! You are not fit to live. You was born and raised in a free country and allowed yourself to be bought for money by the minion of a ruling monarch, to persecute and possibly deliver up to the executioner a man who had committed no crime and had done nothing but what every person with a spark of honor would have done under like circumstances. Understand, villain! Before you breathe out your dog-soul, that, if I had attacked the lieutenant and he had killed me, me, a common citizen, but a man of some value to mankind, his breast would today be adorned with medals, and the fellow would brag about the deed and the so-called highborn ladies would worship him for it. The citizen, however, had to flee. He was robbed of all that was dear to him. That there are individuals who, though born as free citizens of a republic, for which their fathers shed their blood, sink so low as to perform the service of sleuths for European JUNKERS, to hound and deliver to the gallows men seeking rest and security on the soil of this republic, is, to put it mildly, pitiable. Such wretches must die." So saying, Dr. Weber dispatched Bill with the pistol which he had wrested from the latter's hands.

At this moment a young girl with a rifle in her hand stepped out of the bushes and asked herself: "How many more victims will the fellow by the grace of God demand?"

Dr. Weber kicked aside the corpse of the sleuth and threw away the pistol. The young lady gazed motionless on the scene. What a difference between her and the angel who consoled the old woman so heartily on the preceding afternoon!

"Come, child, the number has now reached eight," the doctor said and walked with the young lady to the mysterious wigwam. His carriage was erect and his gait firm. At the wigwam he turned about towards the scene of the bloody encounter just closed and said: "They will not even let us alone in the forest depths among savages. Not enough that they drove me out of my accustomed spheres in my home country, — where my knowledge and experience could be of service to humanity— , they persecute me everywhere. I thought of surrendering myself to the courts instead of defending myself and striking down the stupid fellow when he sought to take me prisoner, but, O heavenly Father! Where should I look for justice? Justice! Humanity raves continually about justice, but never about power."

The girl, who had stepped nearer the doctor in the darkness, rested her fair head against his shoulder. The old man, who a few moments ago had slain a man, had his arm about her neck, and the very hand that ended the sleuth's life encircled the girl's chin. They appeared to be great friends and entertained no regret for the terrible deed. In a cordial tone Dr. Weber said: "Come into the wigwam, child. We must get ready to depart. Today we were again driven from a piece of earth, where we lived simply and peaceably and molested nobody. This tract is now without our fault, steeped in blood. Let us depart as soon as possible, never to return here, although I took great delight in coming here every fall. After crossing the Manitowoc River, we will be with our tribe, the savages, the only men who are faithful after you have once won their hearts. Come, child, let us consider. The earth was today freed of four rowdies and highway men."

As was ascertained subsequently, Shepard and Bill Stuart (the latter even an educated man) were members of a notorious band of outlaws known as the Morgans. The American is always practical. He hires such characters to send them, like bloodhounds, in pursuit of men. Irish immigrants furnish a large contingent to the rowdies in America.

A number of Indians were silently hurrying to their wigwams. They seemed to be in haste, like craftsmen and laborers who hurry home after a hard day's work. They were looking for rest.

The village soon became absolutely quiet again. Only the brook continued to murmur and lament.

XIX. THE GRAVE ON THE RAPPAHANNOCK.

After an exciting and bitter campaign, the citizens of the United States, on November sixth, 1860, elected as president Abraham Lincoln of Illinois the Republican candidate. The South viewed this result as a menace to all its plans. It viewed it as a final rejection of all its plans. The election had promoted disharmony throughout the country. The people of the South alone seemed to be of one mind, with the exception of Western Virginia, where about two thousand Republicans had voted for Lincoln and Hamlin.[67]

The unanimity of the people of the South confirmed it in its intention, which it had long harbored, to secede entirely from the union of states. It was unwilling to lose the sway it had been accustomed to exercise.

The South understood perfectly well that as soon as it had lost the predominant power in the government, the further extension of slavery would have become impossible, and that it was a mere matter of time when the system of slavery existing within its borders would also fall, because it was unnatural, immoral and repugnant to the spirit of the times. In order to avoid these contingencies, the southern states decided to secede from the United States and establish a confederacy of their own, thereby defying public opinion in the northern states.

The result of the election had scarcely been announced, when the legislature of South Carolina issued a call for state convention to be held at the capital, Columbia, on December 17. Its avowed object was the adoption of resolutions favoring secession. At the same time laws were passed to put the state in a preparation for war to give weight to the resolutions about to be adopted. The state army was to consist of ten thousand men.

When, on November tenth, the newly-elected governor Francis W. Pickens was inaugurated, he said in his address that the Republican Party of the North threatened the peace and existence of the South. He laid special stress on the fact that South Carolina had joined the Union as an independent state and only as a result of great pressure brought to bear upon it, for the mutual protection of all the states, and that now, as a sovereign state and because protection had degenerated into oppression it had the right to sever its relations with the Union.

If President James Buchanan had not been a state's rights man in the widest sense of the word, he could have, as President Jackson once did before him, extinguished in the bud the desires of the southern states to secede. He, on the contrary, seemed to favor the confederacy.

[67] West Virginia would, in fact, secede from Confederate Virginia and become its own state in 1863 and was admitted to the Union during the Civil War.

South Carolina at once took possession of the federal offices, the arsenal and Forts Pinckney and Moultrie in the harbor of Charleston. The latter for was occupied by Major Anderson with about eighty union troops. When he found that he could not hold that fort, he withdrew to Fort Sumter; where on April 1, 1861, the booming of big guns inaugurated the bloody war of the rebellion.

The only important question of the big war was whether the North or the South was to be the dominant factor in the Union. The pretexts as to the poor slaves were political tricks calculated to enthuse the great mass of the people. If the southern states had retained their power, one after the other would have been opened up to slavery.

In order to break the power of the slave states, the Republican Party was formed. Human slavery was the issue, the solution of which cost myriads of lives and billions of dollars.

During that period of the civil war following the bombardment of Fort Sumter, the commanders of the volunteer armies of the North were mostly favored politicians who had not the faintest idea of military tactics. Wirepullers and tricksters of all shades crept into positions of responsibility with high salaries attached. Our Mr. Behl, for instance, became colonel of a Wisconsin regiment as a reward for voting in a Republican state convention against Governor Salomon, a German American, whom most of his constituents favored.

Behl controlled two votes in the convention. The fight for the nomination was a hot one. The rabid, know nothing Yankee element set all wheels in motion to force out of office the German Salomon (a namesake of our Indian chief), although he had proved himself a creditable executive officer. To the disgrace of the Germans, be it said that Behl allowed himself to be misled to betray the trust that his constituents had placed in him. The two votes controlled by him were just sufficient to defeat the German-American Governor Salomon for a renomination.

Behl became colonel of the Forty-fifth Wisconsin Infantry Regiment, although he had never before handled either a sword or a gun.[68] His commission was the reward for his base treason. It was issued to him immediately after the convention adjourned. From that time on, he drew pay as a colonel of a regiment that was not yet in existence. The patriot had to see to it that he got a regiment together. Behl finally succeeded in doing so, after he had appointed half a dozen of his relatives to positions as officers. The war was then about ended. Yet Behl went south with his regiment at the country's expense.[69] There were thousands of such creatures in the northern armies. Nearly all of that calibre played havoc with human life and the fund ground out the farmer and the laborer.

---

[68] Belitz had served previously as Captain of Company K of the Wisconsin 9th west of the Mississippi, but it is unclear whether he participated in any fighting

General McClellan's campaign with his large and well-equipped Army of the Potomac proved failures. Since 1861 he lay with the 130,000 men at Centerville and Manassas. Opposing him were only 50,000 Confederates under that great and extraordinarily able leader, General Robert E Lee. McClellan, who could easily have crushed Lee with his superior force, remained inactive, and was later on relieved of his command by President Lincoln.

On January 26, 1863, the Army of Potomac received a new commander in the person of General Joseph Hooker, called "Fighting Joe". He had shown himself to be a brave soldier, but the army and the people were soon to learn that courage and daring alone do not make a general. Hooker was well able to lead a division, but he was not a general. Lee had spent the winter near Fredericksburg, and Hooker on the other side of the Rappahannock. Hooker's forces outnumbered Lee's about two to one.

---

during his time in such role (he was ill and was recruiting for portions of that time).

[69] This aside is a most interesting one, and indicates that the original German version of Yellowbird was published after Henry F. Belitz's death in Kiel on March 31, 1878 given the harshness of the criticisms of Behl (Belitz). Then again, the Chilton press that published the German version of Yellowbird published at least one piece severely critical of Belitz during his time as an officer in the military (Belitz was firmly Republican). Belitz did ultimately serve as colonel of the 45th Wisconsin Infantry (which emerged in November of 1864 and was present only for the Battle of Nashville in December 1864, the functional end of major hostilities in the Western theater of the conflict) but only after serving as a captain in the 9th Wisconsin Infantry, which saw action in the Trans-Mississippi West theater in Missouri, Kansas and Arkansas. Reinhardt Schlicting – who was seemingly both Belitz's brother-in-law (brother to Belitz's wife Helen) and son-in-law (husband of Belitz's daughter Bertha, Bertha having been Belitz's daughter by his first wife) - served as Captain of Company A of the Wisconsin 45th. Belitz was active politically; he served as a member of the Electoral College in 1864, casting a Republican vote for Abraham Lincoln. We have not yet undertaken any research on Belitz's specific, ostensible actions at the 1864 Wisconsin Republican convention mentioned here by Goeres. It is important to note that Governor Salomon used federal troops to quell the November 1862 Port Washington Draft Riot, which several sources cite as costing him the 1864 nomination. He was succeeded by Governor James T. Lewis.

Hooker occupied a defensive position in such a manner as though the enemy were opposing only his left wing. His right wing, Howard's corps, consisting mostly of Germans, had been assigned by him to an extremely weak position. Hooker was not expecting an attack in that direction. Lee, however, was not the man to fail seeing an advantage. By reconnoitering he found the left wing and the left center of Hooker's army occupying impregnable positions, but the right wing very much exposed. He therefore determined to attack him in the most vulnerable spot. For this purpose his army had to be divided. Jackson, one of his bravest generals, was selected for the maneuver, which required celerity.

At daybreak on the second of May, Jackson, under cover of a dense forest, marched past the Union lines at a mile from them. At nine o'clock in the forenoon he reached a portion of the road where he could be seen by the Union troops. However, as the road at that very place took a turn to the south, Hooker believed that the enemy was retiring. Then Hooker was warned that the enemy might possibly contemplate a flank movement. Hooker ordered General Howard to advance his outposts and keep a watchful eye. Howard did not seem to regard that as necessary. He issued no order to that effect and his men had no suspicion of the proximity of the foe. At 3 o'clock in the afternoon Jackson had completed his circuitous march of fifteen miles. He stood only six miles from the position he occupied in the morning and at the other extremity of the Union lines. Two miles from Howard's lines he formed his troops. His scouts reported that Howard's corps had stacked arms and were busy getting their dinner. It is questionable whether such a large body of troops was ever so thoroughly surprised by an enemy in broad daylight. Several brigades had sentinels on duty but no outposts had been placed anywhere. Jackson did not permit this favorable opportunity to escape him. At 5 o'clock he fell with his whole force upon the unsuspecting, bewildered foe. The entire corps was put to route with the exception of fragments of the Second and Third divisions, commanded by Generals Steinwehr and Schurz, who made an attempt to arrest the progress of the enemy. Fortunately General Pleasanton with two cavalry regiments and a mounted battery was in the vicinity and threw himself against the rebels. He found about twenty other cannon, which were loaded with grape and canister and aimed low. He succeeded in opposing the enemy's progress until Hooker was able to throw Berry's division against Jackson's forces and bring these to a halt.

In the mean time Lee had moved to the left, united his troops with those of Stuart and attacked Chancellorsville. Lee had about 42,000 men under his command. Opposed to him were Sickles, French and Slocum with about 32,000 men. Not two miles from these were Meade, Reynold and Howard with 42,000 men. These heard the battle raging, but did not send a man to aid their comrades.

Sickle's corps resisted five charges of the enemy and then was forced to retreat, whereupon General Conch assumed the supreme command of his own accord, apparently for the particular purpose of ordering a retreat to a position selected by Hooker the night previous.

Rain had caused the river to rise. One of the bridges built by Hooker had been swept away and the other was damaged. The second bridge was repaired with the remnants of the first. Aided by darkness of night and the bad weather Hooker fled over this bridge with his 70,000 men before an enemy less then half that number. Poorer and more blundering movements are unknown in the history of warfare.

Not far from the banks of the Rappahannock, where Howard's corps were located, which, as has just been told, suffered severely because of the unpardonable ignorance of Generals Hooker, Meade, Reynolds and especially Howard himself, a handsome young woman was seen. She looked pale and fatigued. She wore a dark dress. An embroidered ribbon was flung over her shoulders and held a field flash. In her arms she held the head of a strong young man with blond, thick hair and beard.

"You will not die, Fritz! You most assuredly not die. One of the wounds is far from your good heart and the others almost of no significance, mere flesh wounds. Take courage, Fritz! You will not die," she said.

From time to time she tried to give the heavily-wounded Union soldier some liquor. After a while he opened his eyes. His face beamed with joy and love, as he gazed into the woman's noble features and told her in a scarcely audible voice: "No, sweet girl! My dear, Birdie! How can I die when you are near? I dare not die. I must live for your sake, for I belong to you. But, child, will you not take cold? Birdie, it is raining hard."

"Until the moment I found you, I had a blanket wrapped about me," she said. "Two friends are using it to make a stretcher of it for you. I have secured for you quarters in the neighborhood of Chancellorsville where I will nurse you like a prince."

The wounded man interrupted her, saying: "Birdie, do you remember that night, in which it rained so hard? It was just four years ago today. Today is May fourth 1863. It was on May 4, 1859, when you displayed such heroism at the breaking of the dam. Do you recollect, Birdie?"

"Yes, certainly I know it. How could I love you so boundlessly, if I had forgotten all that? What has not all happened in those four years, Fritz? Tomorrow it will be just four years that you called on me in my wigwam, and tomorrow, I hope, you will again be in my wigwam to recover your health," she said.

Fichte was too weak to make a reply, but what expressions of love and gratitude did not stream from his eyes! The rain was pouring down. It had united with the blood which was oozing from the wounds in his breast in forming clots on his uniform, and was flowing down his body in a pale red stream. Fichte had again closed his eyes and Yellowbird attempted to bind up his wound more firmly with another bandage.

Fichte, half asleep, was dreaming and murmuring: "At the brook you took leave of me, Birdie. It was such fine weather, Birdie, do you hear the babbling brook? Will you take leave of me again? But not forever, Birdie, not forever; for I cannot be without you. Do you hear how the brook admonishes us to part? You always accompanied me to the brook."

Two men with a stretcher appeared. The field was filled with the dead and the wounded. Sounds of pain and agony were heard everywhere. How terribly cruel is man! Unknown to each other without ever having done each other the least wrong, men fell upon each to murder and mutilate each other.

"The wounded man must be taken out of the morass; it is high time," Yellowbird said calmly, but decidedly to the men "we will soon be relieved. You will not be reproached. I have looked after all."

Yellowbird conducted the heavy task. Fichte had sunk deep in the mire, yet they succeeded in helping him to the stretcher. Yellowbird examined the bandages which appeared to be in good condition. The flow of blood was abated.

The porters were two strong negroes secured by Yellowbird. They were the property of a Mrs. Jones, whose husband perished as major of a Confederate regiment at the battle of Bull Run two years previously.

Yellowbird was drenched; yet she paid as little attention to it as she had done in that eventful night of four years ago, for a greater prize — her all — was at stake. The negroes and Yellowbird took large strides. From time to time they halted in order to enable Yellowbird to inspect Fichte's wounds. It was necessary to prevent the blood from flowing afresh. Yellowbird grasped the opportunity to moisten his lips with the brandy whenever a brief stop was made.

Fichte looked very pale. He was in the midst of a profound slumber. Poor Yellowbird! Still so young and yet how experienced! They had to cover a distance of about four miles. When they had proceeded halfway, they were met by two negroes whom Mrs. Jones had sent to relieve the bearers of the stretcher.

Yellowbird had just placed her hand on Fichte's heart which she found to be still beating. "How long," she asked "will this faithful, noble heart, continue to beat?" The negroes approached the goal with rapid strides. Mrs. Jones, a strong woman of only twenty-eight years, had provided for all. Her family physician, an old man of seventy-eight, was in waiting. He had offered his professional services to his country, but on account of his advanced age they were thankfully declined. Wherever an opportunity presented itself, he employed his skill and knowledge. He had been the family physician of the Jones family for many years. Judging from his name — Louis Bovier — he must have been of French descent. Although he was not attached to the army, he assisted wherever he could. In the past few years he had more cases like the one before him now than he had treated in all his previous career.

Although Mrs. Jones had known Yellowbird but a short time, she had nevertheless grown much attached to her. She frequently went to the neighboring city of Fredericksburg to make purchases and lay in a stock of supplies, for it could not be foreseen whether her home would be cut off or not from traffic with other places.

In Chancellorsville, a small place, there was rejoicing; in Fredericksburg, a considerable town there was more rejoicing. It was caused by the report that Lee with his few men had again annihilated an army of the Potomac. It was not yet known that the brave Stonewall Jackson had been accidentally shot by his own men while he was reconnoitering the movements of his enemy. This event was kept secret as long as possible. When it finally became known, it filled the entire South with deep gloom. He was mourned as one of her greatest heroes.

Fichte found himself under the care of a physician in a well-furnished room. Mrs. Jones had to remind Yellowbird to look after herself, and insisted upon her changing clothes at which she was assisted by one of Mrs. Jones' female slaves. After the experienced doctor had cleaned and probed Fichte's wound, he ventured the opinion that the patient might possibly recover. Very much, he said, depended on the care he received. He knew that able nursing would not be lacking. He did not consider it imperative to remove the bullet at once. Yellowbird heaved a deep sigh of relief. She knew that her affianced possessed a robust constitution. The four intervening years appeared a very long time to her.

Yellowbird was always at Fichte's bedside. He was mortally wounded, in the enemy's country, and entirely dependent upon her. The news of the victory had caused great rejoicing in the village. Old men, women and children were engaged in noisy merrymaking. With the exception of the blacks, no young able-bodied men were to be seen. All men who were able to bear arms were at the front.

Mrs. Jones as well as Yellowbird paid little heed to the noise. The former had been robbed by the war of all that were dear to her save two young sons of tender age. But for these life would to her have been entirely devoid of all purpose. She was perfectly able to perceive what transpired in the breast of her friend. She had soon convinced herself that Miss Weber had received a good education, and that she had come to the distant Virginia to nurse a wounded warrior, was sufficient proof to her that a woman's genuine love was her leading motive. Miss Weber was no adventuress. She was not looking for newspaper notoriety. Mrs. Jones was convinced that Miss Weber was a lady in the true sense of the word and was treated as such by her. She would never otherwise have consented to a Northern soldier being nursed in her house.

Mrs. Jones was the daughter of a wealthy planter by the name of Glaesing, a German from the Rhine Province. Of his three children, Mrs. Jones (Auna) was the eldest, Robert the next, and another daughter the youngest. The Glaesig plantation lay about twenty miles west of Jones place. Although Glaesing was a man advanced in years, he went to war with his son Robert. The bitterness of the planters against the demand of the North knew no bounds. This became evident from the fact that at the presidential election in November 1860 not a single Republican ballot was cast in any southern state with the exception of West Virginia, by factory hands. The hatred of the Confederates towards the Unionists was intense. They could not see with what right interference with their development was sought. The fury of the Confederates reached its climax when Lincoln on January 1, 1863, issued his famous Emancipation Proclamation, which met with a widely different reception in various parts of the country as well as in the army. Many soldiers declared they would not bleed for niggers and a considerable number of officers resigned; — a proof that the liberation of the blacks had nothing to do with the war.

A few years previously Mrs. Jones had been a celebrated beauty. She had received a very high education. What a splendid bridal couple she and William Jones, a tall handsome youth, were! The Glaesing's as well as Jones's had winter homes in Richmond, where they spent a few months of the year. What more could they wish for? They possessed all that man could ask for on earth. Now all that glory and splendor was to be destroyed forever. Mrs. Jones was still a handsome woman. She knew very well what the future had in store for her. She was well versed in the politics of the day. A few years ago, with what pleasure she drove in a princely carriage with her husband to his or her parents. From childhood up she was attended by specially trained slaves, and today?

Her only brother Robert had died about eight months before of a wound received in an assault on Fredericksburg which was then being held by Union troops. Her father had been wounded and crippled. Her father-in-law, who almost worshipped her, had died a year ago. The negroes, who had previously never entertained a thought of disobedience, became unruly. A portion of them had been enlightened about the consequences of Lincoln's proclamation. That the latter gave them their freedom was no secret to them. Many of the slaves considered it an act of kindness on their part to keep on laboring for their masters. The lash was all that held most of them still in check. Hitherto they had heard of the victories of the southern armies only. Of the country and its affairs they had no better idea then the mules with whom they toiled.

In her sorrows Mrs. Jones was glad to have come across Yellowbird. Dr. Bovier had reentered the room to look after his patient. He said little save that the wound would have produced instant death if it had been two inches lower down. Yellowbird was too prudent to molest him with useless questions.

Fichte had a very high fever which was caused chiefly by the wound in the breast. He had been also wounded in two places in the right leg. The latter were so called flesh wounds. Yellowbird did not leave her lover's bedside. He looked pale one hour and flushed the next. It was the fifth of May. Four years ago on that day Fichte had called upon her the last time in Wisconsin's dense forest.

Fichte's face was glowing like fire and heavy drops of perspiration stood on his forehead. Yellowbird had seized his hand and occasionally handed him a powder which Dr. Bovier had left. After a while Fichte opened his eyes and glared about him. Yellowbird wiped his face.

"Birdie," he lisped, after having eyed all the objects in the room; "Birdie, is not to-day the fifth of May?" After she had answered him in the affirmative he continued: "Ah, my Birdy, my sweet Birdie, what a day was that, when I was your guest! With what joy did I not perform my work on the day following! What do I feel? Soon thereafter you left, you wandered farther and farther into the forest recesses, and I became very sad."

Fichte attempted to draw the sweet girl closer to him. Yellowbird bent over him to spare him all the effort. Profound bliss beamed from the eyes of the wounded man who said to her. Birdie, I would cheerfully have built a wigwam for you, in which you and I could have spent our lives together, you as my dear wife and I as your beloved husband. That day, by the brook, you said to me 'Fritz, do not press marriage until I reveal my secret to you. As soon as I announce to you who and what I am, then you may take me whither soever your wish; then I am thine.' The civil war came, but not your explanation. As a citizen and son of this country, I could not withhold my services. I enlisted, as I wrote to you, dear Birdie, at the time. But that you, dear angel was hovering so near to me, I did not know until I received your kind letter. Birdie, even at this day I will not ask who and what you are. I have no right to know it. I know something and that is sufficient. It is that you are good and kind and my darling."

Although this was more than Fichte had spoken at any time since he was wounded, he did not appear to be very much fatigued by it. Yellowbird replied deeply affected; "Fritz! The day is equally important to both of us. My secret concerning the wigwam and myself has cost blood. I was partly educated in the old country. My name is Meta Weber. In that mysterious wigwam I kept my uncle, Konrad Weber, concealed. Now, Fitz, you know all."

"Birdie!" Fritz exclaimed, "you remain my Birdie. Child! I had not expected that. Ah, good God! Konrad Weber also a revolutionary like my good father, who for years is resting under the sod! Differences of opinion, honor and possessions, selfishness and cupidity! Birdie, how much suffering can not be traced to these qualities of men. When I received the first consignment of dainties in camp, especially the pumpernickel, I knew it was my angel that sent it. Otherwise I have no one in the wide world. Birdie, let me thank you for all the good you have done me! How can I return it?"

"That you recover, Fritz," she said; "more I do not ask for."

Fritz, who was still holding Yellowbird's hand, gazed at her trustfully and cheerfully and said: "Yes, I will recover, and then I will lead you — ."

"Yes, Fritz," Yellowbird interrupted him "wherever thou wilt, for now I am thine."

"When my faithful dear uncle was dead and my good Indians were gone, then, Fritz! I had none left but you. When all the ties that bound me to the Indians and to my uncle were severed, I was bound to be near you. I always knew where you were and how you were getting on. But since you were tied down as I had formerly been, I had to avoid a personal meeting with you. But now we are together again and will remain so."

She did not wish him to unduly excite himself and aggravate his condition. He closed his eyes and his pale feature gradually turned scarlet. The crisis of the disease, which was to decide the fate of the two good people, had not yet come. Mrs. Jones stepped into the room as softly as possible. Yellowbird stepped up to her and whispered that the patient had again relapsed into slumber. Weeping, she gave expression to her strong desire that the wounded man might recover. Mrs. Jones replied: "Miss Weber, be prepared for the worst. The pleasure in case of his recovery will be so much the greater. One accustoms oneself to all, even to grief. Oh, if I could only have nursed my William, my dear, good William. After he had bidden me and the children adieu, I never saw him again Miss Weber, think of me and my sad future. All that we possessed was sacrificed for our cause, for our good cause. Our plantations were devastated, our laboring force was taken from us, and frequently incited to rob and murder its former master. In a short time I will be alone and disconsolate with my two boys in a devastated country."

"Such will not be the case, Mrs. Jones," Yellowbird interrupted; "even though I can offer you none but my poor aid, you shall not feel deserted. I will stay with you."

"No, Miss Weber," Mrs. Jones replied; "I cannot demand that you, a young, cheerful girl, should attach yourself to a family which is bowed down with grief and sorrow and has to eke out a miserable existence in a plundered land. I would not make you unhappy, too."

Yellowbird answered: "You permitted me to bring my betrothed into your home. You sent your slaves to my assistance. You relieved me while nursing a mortally wounded man who fought in the ranks of your foes. You did this all from your own free will. Out of my own free will I will stay with you. In case my Fritz should recover, he will, of course, determine our future. You will, in that case, have two faithful friends."

Mrs. Jones clasped her friend in her arms. She felt that she was not entirely alone. She had friends even in the enemy's country, where she had surely not looked for them.

Toward evening the old surgeon returned. He found the two women, like two sisters, at the bedside of the patient. Expecting the crisis, he at once proceeded to another diagnosis. Fichte seemed to be wholly unconscious. Only occasionally, when the doctor probed the wound, he gave signs of life.

The doctor said: "An inflammation, which I expected yesterday and the result of which will decide over life and death, is coming on." Turning to Yellowbird, he said: "Miss, in case the patient should fully regain consciousness, put your affairs with him in order, if there be anything to be done in that line. In such cases we can promise nothing. Change his cold wraps as often as possible, for all depends now upon keeping down the temperature of his body. Internal remedies are not much avail in such severe cases, because the organism is not in a normal condition. The crisis may come within an hour. The outcome will be manifest before tomorrow morning at the latest. Our surgeons are busy night and day. The recent battle in the wilderness has cost thousands of lives. Countless numbers were wounded. Churches, schools, sheds and barns are filled with the wounded. And the continual rain! I must be gone. As long as my feeble bones will carry me, I will not deprive my country of my services. I cannot do anything else for your patient. It is not difficult to heal the wound. See to it that there is no lack of cold wraps!" So saying, the old physician took his departure.

Yellowbird did all in her power to bring her lover back to health. She could not be induced to leave his side even for a moment. Mrs. Jones faithfully assisted her.

At half past nine o'clock in the evening Fichte's mind began to wander. It could not get away from the murmuring brook in distant Wisconsin. Audibly he muttered: "Yes, Birdie, and then you are mine. You are a German and no Indian. You have protected from persecution your foster father, your good uncle! Birdie, where are you?" At these last words he looked about, although he was holding her hand in his own, once so strong, but now enervated by fever.

"Here I am, my Fritz. I am always with you," Yellowbird whispered affectionately. The patient's mind continued to wander: "Birdie, isn't it so? Four years ago today? Ah, Birdie, when I think of the paradise which then opened itself to view; when you answered my smiles, you sweet faithful girl! The brook in the forest is flowing on, and on, and those, who seemed to cause him so much joy, are gone — gone!"

"Yet together again, Fritz," Yellowbird said. Once more there streamed from the eyes of the young warrior that supernaturally happy glow; which can emanate only from a heart enthused by infinite love. Yellowbird remained collected, loving and calm, while Mrs. Jones heart seemed to break. The two women remained silent, and deep quiet reigned in the room. The crisis had come. Its result was as yet undecided.

In spite of the cold wraps of Fiche's head and chest, his body appeared to be burning up. At a quarter of eleven the sick man raised his head and looked wildly about. In his fever delirium he exclaimed: "Hear how the cannon thunders, Birdie! Don't you see the comrades falling? Oh the terrible butchery! When will it end? How happy are my poor, good parents! They rest peacefully in the earth. They know of no wars, murdering and conflagrations. Birdie, Johanna did put the plumb line into Caqua's hunting-pouch. She was unwilling that I should go to the Indians. She had confessed so to me with tears. Birdie, I have forgiven her all. She said you were so good and wise and I should ask you to forgive her. She had no opportunity to speak to you. We should not think evil of her. She had been but a mere child. Hear, Birdie, hear the cannon boom again! Men are being killed!"

"Calm yourself, Fritz, lie down again, my dear boy, you are getting tired. You must have fresh wraps on your chest," Yellowbird consoled him. Yet in spite of the tenderness of her words, Fichte did not seem to understand them. His gaze grew wilder, his body became convulsed and he said: "Birdie, our friend Johanna will and must know, whether you have forgiven her. She rests for more than a year under the earth. I must let her know. I promised it to Johanna."

Contrary to all expectation, Yellowbird had thus far borne up bravely. She was bound to have her lover gaze into an unconcerned face. But at least she collapsed under the strain and amidst a flood of tears she embraced him, sobbing: "Fritz, I have forgiven her, the good girl. I have entertained no grudge against her, I have pitied her, Fritz, for she has loved and suffered."

Fichte placed his arm about Yellowbird and whispered as though nothing ailed him: "Birdie, I knew it, Johanna will be glad if I tell her that. Birdie! How good you are! Poor Birdie! You find no rest. You are always the one to suffer, even when evil-minded and covetous persons wage war against one another. Hear, child! How they shoot and yell and the drums beat!"

Beseechingly Yellowbird replied: "Dear Fritz! Lie down again will you? Your Birdie begs you. You shall recover! You must recover!"

The patient answered: "Yes, yes, Birdie, and then we will saunter together to the brook in the forest depths. I will place my arm about you and you will rest your dear head on my breast. Your head has laid where I now feel such racking, burning pains. There you will again gaze at me, Birdie, with your sweet eyes, and then you will kiss me good-bye, as you did four years ago to-day."

Fichte's voice grew fainter. Yellowbird bent forward over him and covered his mouth with kisses. The pulse-beat of the patient grew faster. The boiling heat of his blood ignited his heart. Fichte convulsively raised his body and said: "Birdie, you must not cry. See, I do not cry. I am improving. Birdie, it was four years ago today Birdie, you must not cry."

The warrior had uttered his last words. His head felt back upon the cushion. A few moments later he raised his hand and immediately dropped it again. The crisis was over — Fichte was dead.

It was again the fifth of May. The year of 1867. Two women in black were approaching a cemetery. Each of them held by the hand a sprightly boy. The cemetery, which was small, had the appearance of a little paradise. The women opened the gate of the cemetery with a key. The cemetery contained but a few graves and was surrounded by an iron fence. The remains of the members of but a few families rested there. The headstones were all alike. One grave only had a supplementary ornament in the shape of a tiny, gold bird. The massive marble pedestal bore the inscription: "Freidrich Fichte, died May 5, 1863. From his bride, Yellowbird."

The monuments above the other dead were dedicated to the memory of relatives of Mrs. Jones. By ceaseless efforts Mrs. Jones, with Yellowbird's aid, succeeded in finding the remains of her good William. They now reposed near those of Fichte. Mr. Glaesing and Mrs. Jones' parents also rested there.

The little cemetery, which contained only five graves, occupied a hummock, past which a rivulet flowed, which emptied into the Rappahannock two miles from Chancellorsville. The eldest of the two boys clung to the woman who cried bitterly — Yellowbird. She was to take an eternal farewell from a spot that was sacred to her, the burial place of her lover, Fritze Fichte. It became difficult for her to leave the grave. The boy sobbed with her. He, too, had become very fond of her, his preceptress in music. Mrs. Jones also was loath to leave the grave of her William. For the last time Yellowbird embraced the monument with the golden bird and voiced her sorrow thus: "Fritz! O Fritz! I must leave thee now. Your Birdie will never more weep over your grave. She must go far, far away, to Brazil. Other hands will plant flowers on your grave, paid hands, Fritz! I must go. You remain here all alone, far away from your parents, the sole relatives you had. And now thy Birdie goes likewise. She must go, for the good woman, in whose house you was nursed, wanders away too."

Plucking some flowers she had planted on Fichte's grave, she exclaimed amid a stream of tears: "Fritz, my darling! My beloved betrothed! Repose undisturbed! The rivulet stays here. It will eternally murmur to you of the love, the great love of your Birdie, who leaves you forever."

A carriage came along and halted at the entrance of the graveyard. It was a sister of Mrs. Jones and her husband. She was her sole surviving blood relative. Mrs. Jones' sister married a good German who had purchased the plantation of the Glaesings and rented that of Mrs. Jones, who was about to depart for Germany with her two sons. Her father there had a small estate that his brother, Adam Glaesing, took care of. Mrs. Jones' father had never claimed the estate, because he had more than he needed in the United States. Uncle Adam was unmarried and had invited Mrs. Jones and the children to sojourn with him, as the estate yielded enough to shield them all. The boys could obtain a good education in the vicinity of Dusseldorf and remain in Germany until the sad state of affairs in their desolate home had changed for the better.

Mrs. Jones saw that it was best thing she could do for her children. In accordance with Yellowbird's special wish, their departure was fixed for the fifth of May, exactly four years after Fichte, the betrothed of her bosom friend, had died. Yellowbird had received her heritage, which was considerable, and had always assisted Mrs. Jones, even against the latter's wishes. She had caused all the monuments in the little graveyard to be made and had paid for them.

Heinrich Duering, Mrs. Jones' brother-in-law, and his wife had undertaken the obligation of caring for the cemetery, for which purpose Yellowbird had left a sufficient sum. Young Mrs. Duering had long since acquainted herself with housework. She had learned to forget to have slaves for her and attend to her toilet. Her once snow white and tender hands had accustomed themselves to manual labor. Her husband led with the good example. Henrich Duering came from Holstein and was accustomed to work from childhood up. On a trip from Ohio to Virginia to look up a countryman of his, he rented a plantation and became acquainted with Martha Glaesing who soon thereafter became his wife.

Four years Yellowbird had been besought to return to Brazil by a brother of her deceased mother. At the time that her father brought her to Germany, he was pursuing his studies there. He urged her to make her home with him, as she had no relatives either in Germany or North America.

After Mrs. Jones had decided to go to Germany, Yellowbird had finally resolved to accept her uncle's invitation and return to Brazil. Her uncle was a well-to-do business man of Para[70] and was married to a French woman, whom he portrayed to be of excellent character.

Mrs. Jones was already at the carriage. Yellowbird, bowed down with grief, came slowly along, leaning on the boy. At the gate she paused a moment and whispered in scarcely audible tones:

"Today it is eight years since I took leave of you — at the brook — took leave of you — dear Fritz! Farewell! Farewell! Thou dear, good Fritz! Farewell! Birdie goes away." A flood of tears burst from those once beautiful eyes. How she had aged! Heinrich Duering locked the gate of the little cemetery. At the carriage, Yellowbird's eyes roamed once more over the surrounding country. Beneath her the Rappahannock was slowly wending its way to the Chesapeake Bay.

The gloomy forests of the Wilderness, where the awful carnage of four years previously had taken place, lay close before her[71]. There, too, her Fritz, her all, had been laid low by a murderous missile. Her Fritz, who rested here so peacefully, so all alone! All eyes were moist and the young Walter even cast an anxious look at her.

Duering tenderly assisted Yellowbird into the carriage, where the others had already seated themselves, and the company set out on its journey to Baltimore via Fredericksburg.

Yellowbird's steamer left two days before the vessel that was to convey Mrs. Jones to Europe. The two friends found it very hard to leave each other. The young Walter sobbed piteously. The officers finally conducted Yellowbird to the boat. It was high time. The floating colossus was about to depart.

On the quarterdeck there stood a pale, wan girl who waved a final farewell with her handkerchief, while little Walter, who with his mother was watching the departure of the vessel from the shore was weeping bitterly. His mother was too much occupied with her own sorrow and could not console him.

After a short time nothing remained visible of the boat except a cloud of smoke leaving the funnels of the big ship, and it too soon vanished from the sight of the little group.

Poor Birdie!

---

[70] The chief city of this state, located at the mouth of the Amazon River in South America, is Belém.

[71] The Battle of the Wilderness, fought May 5-7, 1864; accordingly, this should be three years earlier – not four.

XX. CONCLUSION.

The devastated and plundered Confederate states, once the abode of wealth and splendor, could not rally. Their proud inhabitants were conquered. Overwhelming forces had crushed them. They had no working force remaining to supply them with victuals, weapons, horses and ammunition.

The so-called civil rights bill had become a law[72]. It gave all former slaves as well as all negroes all the rights and privileges of citizenship. The so-called Freedman's Bureau was created. It was conducted by army officers — chiefly political wire-pullers from the North. A powerful political machine was organized and controlled the nominating conventions and elections in almost all of the southern states.

The ignorant negroes, who until recently had been slaves and possessed not the remotest idea of civil duties, were used as voting cattle by the political tricksters[73]. As the negroes were in the majority in the southern states, those swindlers, or "carpet-baggers", as they were popularly called, could easily capture all governmental offices.

A Republican congress favored those scoundrels. President Grant, under whose administration carpet-bagging flourished most luxuriantly, was too ignorant to see through the game of those sharpers. Such a condition of affairs was not prone to again build up the devastated and vanquished South.

At the start, President Johnson opposed this policy, which gave rise to so much friction. If the awful whiskey frauds[74] are also taken into consideration, one can truthfully say that Grant administration was the poorest and most corrupt the United States had ever seen.

---

[72] This appears to be a reference to the Civil Rights Act of 1866.

[73] Again, Goeres' views do not seem to account for brilliant African American congressmen elected during Reconstruction, such as Roberts Smalls and Robert Brown Elliott, or black majority state constitutional conventions that produced significant state consitutions.

The noble Lincoln, who died before the war was wholly concluded, had decided, sensible plans of reconstruction. With him the good principles of the Republican Party perished.[75]

On the right bank of the Wisconsin River, about twenty miles above Wausau, lies the spot where the Chippewa Indians always pitched their wigwams in the summer time, especially on account of the wild rice fields[76]. Indians are rarely seen there at this day.

The few preserved by fate were consigned along with other tribes to reservations where they are fast approaching total extinction. A single log cabin remained standing near the spot referred to, where once the Chippewas held sway and had many a merry time. In this cabin there dwelt alone for many years a terribly homely fellow — a gigantic Indian. He seemed to enjoy special privileges. He owned two lively ponies which years ago were captured from highwaymen. Another pony was his favorite and was especially well taken care of by him. It was a little black pony called Robin.

About five hundred paces from the cabin was a sand hill, which in very remote times had perhaps been the bed of the Wisconsin River. This sand lot contained a number of hummocks some of which had partially collapsed. One of the little mounds was tolerably well preserved. It even seemed as though flowers had once upon a time grown on it. A tombstone on the mound bore the legend: "Here rests Dr. Konrad Weber among the savages who were his most faithful friends."

The log cabin is now uninhabited. Robin and the other ponies are gone. The giant was one day found dead near the grave of Dr. Weber. To Caqua's breast was attached a not saying: "Good people bury me to the right of Dr. Weber, Banker Nash will pay you well for your trouble." These words had been written many years ago, by a woman who had also looked to it that the sand-lot in question had been recorded as cemetery to be protected from the sacreligious hands of the greedy.

Caqua, the giant, had faithfully obeyed the dictates of his goddess. He would have obeyed them at the expense of his life.

Every month Mr. Nash handed the giant ten dollars as well as other things.

---

[74] The Whiskey Ring Scandal of 1875, which involved diversion of tax payments by Midwestern distillers, tarnished the Ulysses S. Grant administration – but which was also ended through the efforts of Grant's administration.

[75] Goeres was clearly not a fan of Reconstruction or the Radical Republicans that controlled Congress at the time.

[76] This would put the spot just north of Merrill, Wisconsin.

In spite of his frightful appearance, Caqua was respected by the members of his tribe, for he had a good advocate.

The man of the mysterious wigwam was found dead one morning. To the Queen of the Chippewas he bequeathed a number of well-assorted papers, about which Caqua knew. However that Dr. Weber had committed suicide, Caqua did not know.

After Yellowbird had arrived at the age of twenty-one, Dr. Weber did not wish to chain the girl to his fate any longer. He could not bear the idea, solely to guard his frail body in a miserable world, to withhold her natural rights from a blooming young girl. No, much his life was not worth.

Through his efforts Yellowbird had received an education second to that of no young woman in the state of Wisconsin. The good doctor felt that he had thus to some degree made amends for the many sacrifices the dear child had made for him. He would for nothing in the world have again raised his hand to kill an assailant. He had shed more blood than he wished. That life of his, which had been so much sought for and which he always courageously defended, he finally brought to a close, with a cold smile, by a few grains of poison. Yellowbird was to remain in ignorance of his final undertaking. After his demise, she remained queen of her faithful savages until these were forced, by virtue of a treaty concluded between their representatives and the government, to either move on a reservation or forego government aid. On the reservation the Indians were supplied with farming implements and given instructions in their use by government employers. Nature has not, however, intended these people for agriculture. The older ones among them soon wandered off into their Happy Hunting Grounds. Only the younger ones survived.

The day on which Yellowbird and the Indians took final leave of each other is commemorated as follows in the diary of an eye witness: "Again and again Pona, Meeme and the other children flew into Yellowbird's arms. The elder Indians rolled on the ground like sick beasts. The squaws howled in a heart-rending manner. The giant was beside himself."

Kiel is now a flourishing little city. It did not develop into a second Jerusalem, as Mr. Behl had expected.

The mill dam referred to in our tale was totally destroyed by high water in 1881 and rebuilt later by another owner. The sawmill has long since disappeared. It had to make way for a grist mill. The beautiful virgin forests are gone. They have been replaced by fertile grain fields. The brook which floated before Fichte's imagination in his last moments, deserves the name of one after very heavy rains only, for its sources dried up after the destruction of its neighbors, the patriarchs of the forest, exposed it to the withering influences of wind and sunshine. The book, too, was once a denizen of the forest.

The plankroad has long since fulfilled its function and is to-day no better than ordinary roads. Markets are to be found everywhere in Wisconsin at this day. Railroads extend in all directions. In 1872, a railway was built from Milwaukee, with the metropolis of the state linked to Kiel, which is now connected by rail with all places from ocean to ocean.

Behl is dead now for a number of years. Of the many Spanish castles built by him not one has been realized. He died soon after a conflagration destroyed his residence and the bulk of his property, none of which was insured. After his demise, his widow found herself in a bad way financially. Her property finally was gobbled up by conscienceless speculators, of whom one particularly had his fingers deep in the pie.

A certain grocer wormed himself into the confidence of the poor widow by pretending to be anxious to protect and assert her rights. He dissuaded Behl's creditors from asserting to their fullest extent their claims and succeeded in getting them to foreclose on only a portion of the realty. To the creditors he argued: "It is to be hoped that there is nobody on earth, who is desirous of enriching himself at the expense of a widow and her children. We will satisfy our claims with the proceeds of a portion of the estate, in a ratio to our claims, and cancel all claims against the unhappy family."

In the meantime the grocer bought up claims against Behl's estate, which were considered of very little value, for a mere song. As the creditors were desirous or treating the Behl family as generously as possible and as the grocer pretended to be working to the end to save it as large a share of the estate as possible, he was soon in the possession of all claims against the estate. He then began foreclosure proceedings ending with the turning out into the street of the widow and her children. Behl's employees, too were buncoed out of their just share by that enterprising friend of humanity.[77]

About four acres of land, the last possession of the impoverished family, which were situated in the very center of Kiel and are now covered with pretty houses gave rise to a long lawsuit between the grocer and another greedy countryman. These two personifications of integrity fought the tract as two vultures wrangle about carrion.

---

[77] Who is this despised grocer? Is it Charles Heins, first president of the Village of Kiel when Kiel was incorporated as such in 1892…whose home is now the Kiel Area Historical Society house at Fremont and Third?

When the poor widow found that she had been so shamefully deceived, she appealed to the conscience of the grocer! Good Gracious! He had about as much conscience as his barrels, out of which he gave as little as possible for as much as possible. Some weeks later Mrs. Behl had to be taken to an insane asylum. The grief at the base fraud, the worming care for the support of herself and her little ones together with her somewhat exalted sense of honor were sufficient to cloud her mind. Her nervous system was a total wreck.

After a sojourn of six years in the state hospital for the insane she was sent as an incurable to the county asylum, from which she ran away as often as possible. She was always bound to return to Kiel, to regain her property and visit her little ones. Yet there is a remedy for all things. Mrs. Behl was taken from the Manitowoc asylum to that of another county, from which another insane person was transferred to the former asylum.[78] Tit for tat.

Her children, whom Mrs. Behl, while a young and happy mother hardly entrusted long enough to another person to enable her to pay a visit to an Indian village, are now throughout the country. They have all become without exception able and respectable men and women. To accomplish this end, Helen, the eldest of Behl's daughters sacrificed all her prospects in life.[79]

Mrs. Behl, who has become quite ancient, busies herself in the asylum with placing together scraps of paper and studying from them her rights. The land of which her family was robbed is called to this day the "blood-acre".[80]

New Holstein also has grown to be a very pretty little town, surrounded by splendid farms.

---

[78] The Manitowoc Pilot reports that Sheriff Murphy of Manitowoc County "left on Monday for Oshkosh to convey Mrs. Belitz of Schleswig, to the asylum there." on Aug. 18, 1881.

[79] It appears she, too, ultimately went to the asylum.

[80] This would be land at the southwest corner of Fremont and Fourth Streets (Belitz's final residence was the building that is currently MC's Pub & Grill). HELEN CATHERINE BELITZ died in 1910, and is listed in her obituary as having been in the Manitowoc County asylum for 30 years.

Elkhart Lake, where Yellowbird's Indian pupils caught fish when it was still encircled with virgin forest, is a wonderfully pretty sheet of water of about three hundred and fifty acres. It is today one of the most noted watering places in the Northwest. On its banks are clusters of fine hotels and villas, in the midst of paradisiacal parks.[81] Its crystalline, sparkling waters are visited every season by thousands of health and pleasure seekers from all states of the Union, who are delighted with the beautiful surroundings and the fresh, invigorating air.

The German language and song are cultivated to this day in New Holstein as well as in Kiel. Nearly all of the revolutionaries, who in the forties and fifties settled in those quarters and to whom the present generation is indebted to for so much, are now gone to their eternal repose.

The hearts which once beat so warmly are still. Here, too, the revolutionaries did not find what they strove for in their German fatherland. Yet their memory will be long kept green, for they founded theaters and musical, singing and turning[82] societies. May they rest in peace!

The great republic of the United States is today the scene of greater oppression then ever before. What the great and far-seeing Lincoln predicted, or rather foresaw, has come true. He said: "Syndicates will be formed and these will obtain control of legislative bodies and even the courts. They will control the market, the railroads, metals, coal, oil and money, and endeavor to oppress the people of this great and splendid republic, the preservation of which as cost so much blood."

Lincoln was right. The people of the United States are at this day bearing greater burdens on their shoulders than ever before.

We are again on the eve of a revolution, perhaps a bloodier one than the world has ever seen.

The calculations of tyrants and vampires have generally proved erroneous, because they left out of consideration the question how much the people can bear. This limit is hard to define.

The Confederate states have not entirely recovered, although they have long since been again received into the sisterhood of states. Cotton and tobacco are now also raised in other states than at the time of the war.

---

[81] Elkhart Lake's grand Victorian resorts emerged between the 1860s and 1890s, but particularly following the arrival of the train in 1872 (the same year the train arrived in Kiel).

[82] Turnverein organizations, German immigrant groups dedicated to physical health, exercise and fraternity.

The woes caused by Grant's satellites, the carpet-baggers, who robbed a vanquished people of even the ruins of their former possessions, have not been entirely overcome. The taxes caused by fraudulent pension laws are excessively onerous.

If our revolutionaries could today emerge from their graves and behold the disgraceful state of affairs, they would soon gladly again sink back into their sepulchers with the conviction that all countries, even republics, have their dark sides and exclaim with Robert Blum: "It takes republicans to make a republic."

*   *   *

A few years ago a circus gave a performance in Manitowoc. Big posters and huge newspaper advertisements announced that it would display more curiosities than any of its predecessors.

The Americans have reached the ne plus ultra in the lines of humbug. They know how to toot their own horn. This is especially true of circus managers. What's the difference if their performances fall short of their announcements? The latter have accomplished their purpose, that of packing the capacity of their show-tents. The circus is for the average American what a bull-fight is to the Spaniard. The stale jests of the clowns always find willing ears and applause. An American will drop all other business to attend a circus performance, even though he may have to journey twenty and even thirty miles to reach it.

The youthful American accompanies "his best girl" to such a show and feels like a victorious hero about it. Like a sighing lover he does not leave his girl out of sight for a moment, but waits upon her as princesses are waited on. Woe to him who dares offer an insult to her!

The sides of sheds and barns, dead walls and fences were plastered over with huge posters in flaring colors and gigantic letters and pictures, explaining all impossible things that would be exhibited and performed in the show. Monsters, mammoths and reptiles in more than life size were adorning the gaudy, house-high placards.

One of the posters contained a picture of a group of Indians, each of whom, according to the announcement, was to be a vocalist of prominence. Their names were given as Kaan, Caqua, Pona, Mensequaw, Sapa, Meeme and Squawqua.

At the base of the poster was printed this legend: The above great Indian artists who will appear in the circus, are the pupils of the queen of the Chippewas, the never-to-be-forgotten

YELLOWBIRD.

Author Henry Goeres with family at his home,
Schloss Luxemburg, in Kiel, Wisconsin.